THE ULTIMATE
MIXER COOKBOOK

THE ULTIMATE
MIXER COOKBOOK

150 INTERNATIONAL RECIPES MADE EFFORTLESSLY

KAY HALSEY

KEY TO KITCHENAID ATTACHMENTS

 wire whip

 flat beater

 dough hook

 food grinder

 strainer

 pasta maker

 sausage stuffer

 juicer

 grain mill

ROTARY SLICER / SHREDDER

 medium shredding drum

 coarse shredding drum

 slicing drum

 fine shredding drum

 stripping drum

 potato grating drum

BLENDER SPEED SETTINGS

blender

stir

chop

mix

purée

liquefy

MEASURES AND ABBREVIATIONS

The following abbreviations have been used in the recipes:

Tbsp = tablespoon
tsp = teaspoon
g = gram
kg = kilogram
ml = millilitre
l = litre
cup = 250 ml

NOTE

All spoon measurements used throughout this book are level unless otherwise specified.

Never mix metric and cup measures in one recipe, use one system or the other.

WARNING

Because of the slight risk of salmonella, raw or lightly cooked eggs should not be served to the very young, the ill or elderly, or to pregnant women.

A QUINTET BOOK

Copyright © 2003 Quintet Publishing Ltd

ISBN 1-86155-378-1

This book was designed and produced by
Quintet Publishing Limited
6 Blundell Street
London N7 9BH

Publisher: Oliver Salzmann
Managing Editor: Diana Steedman
Text editor: Margaret Gilbey, Kay Halsey
Creative Director: Richard Dewing
Design: Janis Utton, Sharanjit Dhol, Tristan de Lancey
Photography: Tim Ferguson Hill, Ian Garlick
Food Styling: Jacqueline Bellefontaine, Christina Rodrigues

Colour separation by Chroma Graphics Pte Ltd, Singapore
Printed in Singapore by Star Standard Industries (Pte) Ltd.

ACKNOWLEDGEMENTS
The Publishers are grateful to the following for assistance, guidance and support provided in the production of this book, especially to Gina Steer, Catherine Atkinson, Elizabeth Ramjoué, Fiona Ford, Mauro Spagnol, Catherine Masciocchi, Katie Bishop, Rosemary Moon, Jenny Stacey, for their work with the recipes; and to Paul Judge for use of his kitchen for photography.

CONTENTS

KITCHENAID®–A LEGEND in professional kitchens and restaurants, the KitchenAid® mixer was developed in 1919 and has stood the test of time to become an American icon. A design classic, its beauty lies in its power and workmanlike efficiency. All-metal, robust and stable, the machine beats, whisks, stirs, kneads and mixes – performing the most repetitive, time-consuming and heavy jobs in the kitchen with a graceful ease.

In 1908, the same year that Henry Ford first produced his Model T, Herbert Johnston, an engineer from Ohio, found himself watching a baker laboriously mixing his bread dough with a heavy iron spoon. The new century had imbued the country with a spirit of enterprise and discovery, and Herbert felt sure he could find a way of mechanizing this heavy work. He began to work on developing what would soon become the world's first commercial mixer.

His first attempt to create a mixer, the Hobart model H, went on the market in 1914 and was a giant, with a huge 75-litres capacity. Its commercial potential was soon realized and eager customers ranged from chains of bakeries to the US Navy, which by 1917 had made it standard equipment on the galleys of all its ships. The success of the H model inspired Hobart's engineers to start thinking about creating a mixer for home use.

During World War I Hobart, along with most other American manufacturers, converted their production lines to war work. So it was not until after the War, on the brink of the peace and prosperity of the Roaring Twenties, that thought turned again to producing a mixer for the home. In 1919, that dream became a reality and the Hobart model H-5, the first domestic mixer, broke on to the market. Named the 'KitchenAid', the model was a direct descendant of Hobart's professional models and a real breakthrough. Of extremely high quality, the KitchenAid® mixers were made with real attention to detail, and only four machines a day rolled off the company's assembly line in Springfield, Ohio. However, the KitchenAid mixer was by no means cheap – priced at $189.50 it cost the equivalent of $1,500 in today's dollars.

Throughout the 1920s, the company continued to make new models, refining the design to deliver the same quality at a lower price. In 1927 they launched their G model, which was to mark the beginning of a new era of significant growth for the company, selling 20 000 models in just three years. Ever glamorous, the new KitchenAid mixer wowed America, and its famous users ranged from Henry Ford to Ginger Rogers and Marion Davies.

Even with the G model doing so well, the Depression in the 1930s forced KitchenAid to keep searching for ways to produce ever better-value models. In a masterful move in 1936, the world-acclaimed designer Egmont Arens was commissioned to create three new models for the company. His K models were to become design icons, winning many awards and earning a place in design museums throughout the world. In 1955, KitchenAid caused a sensation at the Atlantic City Housewares Show when the K model first appeared in a range of colours – Petal Pink, Sunny Yellow, Island Green, Satin Chrome and Antique Copper. It was certainly a far cry from the workmanlike colours of the original machines.

Up to this day, the basic design remains virtually unchanged and the attachments that came with Egmont Arens' 1936 machine could in fact be used in a machine bought today. The current palette of exciting colours was introduced as recently as 1994, and the KitchenAid mixer can now be bought in Imperial Red, Cobalt Blue, Onyx Black, Almond Cream, Majestic Yellow, Matt Grey, Brushed Nickel, Chrome and White.

So what has made the KitchenAid mixer such a classic design and the world's top household mixer?

Just looking at the machine, the first reason is obvious. The KitchenAid mixer is made of solid metal with a tough enamel finish that is made to last. As well as looking good, this means the machine is stable, tough and robust. Initially developed for the workload of busy professional kitchens, KitchenAid mixers are made to be used hard.

Turn on your machine and you'll see the KitchenAid mixer's unique planetary mixing method kick into action. Patented as part of the original 1919 design, the machine looks effortlessly graceful as the flat beater, wire whip or dough hook turns around the mixer bowl, while the planetary turns the opposite way, blending ingredients thoroughly and reaching right into every part of the bowl.

And the force that is making your KitchenAid mixer work so efficiently is its impressive 300 Watts of power, which allows the 10-speed, gear-driven motor to steadily ease you through from gentle stirring to high-speed whipping. The result is a quiet, reliable and efficient machine.

After your cake is in the oven, the KitchenAid mixer's timeless design and smooth, rounded edges make it easy to clean, with no lids or blades to trap food.

But your KitchenAid mixer doesn't stop there. Additional attachments, which fit easily in and out of a single hub, allow the machine to do all the jobs of a food processor and more. Chopping, grating or slicing, you can mince your own meat or grind your own flour, and if you want, your KitchenAid mixer can transform itself into a pasta or sausage maker, a strainer or even your own juicer.

GETTING TO KNOW YOUR KITCHENAID® MIXER

Every time you use your KitchenAid mixer you'll get to know it a little better and learn what it does best. Don't only use recipes written for the KitchenAid mixer – it will speed up almost any food preparation. You can convert all your favourite recipes using just your own observations and experience.

The Speed Control Guide in your manual will help you, and the recipes written especially for the KitchenAid mixer in this book are a good place to start getting a feeling for correct timings and consistencies.

PROFESSIONAL TIPS When mixing, start on the slowest speed and gradually increase to the required speed to prevent too much splashing, especially when there is a large amount of liquid ingredients. Use the Speed Control Guide to help you decide which speed is suitable for each job and attachment. If you are unsure, use a slower speed and work up gradually. Use the Pouring Shield to make adding ingredients while the machine is operating less messy. The KitchenAid mixer is powerful, and you will find that you probably need to adjust down the mixing times in all your recipes to avoid overbeating.

When whisking, start on the slowest speed and gradually increase the speed until the mixture is frothy. You can then increase it further to a fast whisking speed. However, do not whisk too quickly as this will in fact incorporate less air, leading to a dense and heavy mixture. If whisking eggs, make sure they are at room temperature. If whipping cream, chill the mixer bowl first and keep the cream in the fridge until ready to mix. Be careful not to overwhip, as cream can thicken very quickly, and don't use the wire whip for recipes with butter or margarine in them as this can get stuck in the wire whip.

When making bread, you can start by mixing the ingredients together using the flat beater, especially if you're only making a small quantity of dough, as it is more efficient for straightforward mixing than the dough hook. Change to the dough hook to mix in the liquid, adding it gradually so it doesn't form a pool that might slow down the mixing. When the dough starts to form a ball, knead for a few minutes until smooth and elastic. You can just leave the bread to prove in the bowl, covered with the plastic lid, which will pop off when the bread rises.

When adding extra ingredients, add as close to the side of the bowl as possible, not directly into the moving beater (the pouring shield will help you do this). When adding solid ingredients such as nuts, raisins or candied fruits into a batter, always fold them in during the last few seconds of mixing on the slowest speed to prevent the air being knocked out.

When you are not using your machine, leave it on the counter top, storing the three attachments in the bowl with the plastic cover on to keep it all dust-free and ready-to-use.

THE FLAT BEATER The workhorse of your KitchenAid mixer, the flat beater is the attachment to turn to for all kinds of mixing. Able to deal with any normal to heavy mixtures, it is of course great for making cakes, biscuits and pastry, deftly cutting in soft butter or margarine or creaming a mixture. However, the flat beater can mash vegetables or whip up dips and pâtés; evenly blend together meatloaf and meatballs; or stir together a shiny butter cream. Try it for any mixture that needs to be quickly stirred together or thoroughly blended.

THE WIRE WHIP is the attachment to use when you need to incorporate some air into your mixture. It can whip cream; whisk eggs to create meringues, ice creams, mousses and mayonnaise; and is also great for applying a little first-aid to lumpy sauces and custards. Use the wire whip rather than the flat beater when you want to make whisked sponges – light cakes made without fat – and fluffy egg white icings.

THE DOUGH HOOK is for making and kneading doughs. If you want to wake up to the smell of home-made bread, the dough hook can mix and knead any kind, from focaccia to rye; dinner rolls to thin-crust pizzas.. The dough hook is also used to make pasta dough. And if you enjoy baking your own cakes, a great tip is to use the dough hook rather than the beater to stir the fruit and nuts into the cake mix.

ABOVE LEFT: *Rotary slicer/shredder* **ABOVE MIDDLE:** *Food grinder with food tray, strainer and sausage stuffer accessories* **ABOVE RIGHT:** *Grain mill*

ATTACHMENTS AND ACCESSORIES

ROTARY SLICER/SHREDDER This attachment is so useful it is probably used more frequently than any other in the recipes. Store it with the sharp slicing drum in place and it'll be ready to go when you need to slice a few onions for a sauce or some potatoes for a topping. The rotary slicer/shredder comes with three drums: a medium and a coarse shredding drum and a slicing drum. All three are great for making salads, especially coleslaw; slicing potatoes for gratins; shredding fruit for pies; grating cheese; and slicing big quantities of raw or cooked vegetables for cooking. If you need to switch from slicing to shredding in the middle of a recipe, you don't have to remove the attachment from your KitchenAid mixer, just change the drum, and you can even grate straight into the same bowl. The shredding drums can also do thin strips of vegetables – just turn your vegetable around and put it into the machine horizontally.

OPTIONAL DRUMS There are three additional drums for use with the rotary slicer/shredder for more precision slicing and shredding. The fine shredding drum makes light work of cheese, chocolate, nuts and bread, there is a potato grating drum and a stripping drum for julienne-style vegetables.

FOOD GRINDER The food grinder is much more than just a great mincer. This attachment is the equivalent of the main blade in a food processor and it can chop and roughly liquidize as well as grind. Use it, of course, for mincing meat and fish. It allows you to choose exactly the cut and quality you want and has a choice of a coarse or fine grinding plate for making your own charcuterie, from sausages to pâtés, or some high-quality home-made burgers for your barbecue. But use it also to make breadcrumbs or cheesecake bases; shred firm fruit and cheese; grate a carrot very finely or mince an onion to disappear into a sauce. If you want to make a soup or sauce with a rough, country-style texture, use this attachment rather than the strainer. The food grinder is also the body for the strainer and the sausage stuffer.

FOOD TRAY If you process large volumes of fruits, vegetables or meats, the food tray is one accessory you'll definitely want to own. It easily attaches on to the food grinder to provide a much larger capacity to both the grinder and the strainer, allowing you to fill the food tray up with more fruit or vegetables for processing without having to refill so often.

SAUSAGE STUFFER The sausage stuffer attaches to the food grinder and the two work together to produce delicious old-fashioned, home-made sausages and sausage meat that can be made from quality cuts of meat. The sausage stuffer can produce any sausages, not just the classic meat varieties, but vegetarian or uncased ones too. Once made, sausages are quick to cook and make an easy, simple supper.

ABOVE LEFT: *Pasta maker* ABOVE MIDDLE: *Juicer* ABOVE RIGHT: *Can opener*

STRAINER While the food grinder can produce a rough purée, it is the strainer that will break fruit and vegetables down to the smoothest pulp. Attaching to the food grinder, the strainer can purée any soft fruits and cooked vegetables, while separating out pips, stems and skins. It will make a silky smooth soup or sauce, or if you want a bit more texture, you can just mix the smooth and rough pulps back together again. Perfect for preparing large quantities of fruit for a sorbet, coulis or a smooth jelly jam, the strainer allows you to make the most of a summer glut of fresh fruit. It also provides a wonderfully easy way of preparing your own healthy baby food.

JUICER Perfect for preparing large quantities of orange, grapefruit, lemon or lime juice in no time at all for everything from sorbets to marmalade to icy home-made lemonade. So easy to use, you can up your daily fruit intake by creating a healthy juice to drink every day. Kick-start your morning with freshly squeezed orange, or add citrus juice to your favourite breakfast smoothie to make a sensational and healthy sunrise drink.

POURING SHIELD The pouring shield makes adding ingredients while mixing easy. Sitting on the rim of the mixer bowl, the pouring spout directs the food to the sides when adding new ingredients and the shield prevents any splashing. Transparent, it also gives you a full view of the ingredients in the bowl.

PASTA MAKER This beautifully made, traditional-style pasta machine makes daily home-made pasta a reality. Crafted out of chromed metal in Italy by Marcato, who also produce hand-operated machines, it is easy and fun to use. The roller and two cutters allow you to make any kind of flat pasta, from sheets of lasagne to strips of tagliatelle and even threads of angel hair pasta. And it's quick – the flat beater whips up the pasta dough, the dough hook kneads it, then the pasta rollers do all the work while you use both hands to thread the sheets through until they are as smooth, thin and wide as required. The cutters can then cut the sheets into lengths of spaghetti or noodles to be cooked right away.

GRAIN MILL The grain mill transforms your KitchenAid mixer into a new machine – a mill that can grind grains from wheat and rye to rice and corn to produce the freshest flour for baking delicious and nutritious wholegrain breads, muffins and cakes. It can also create more unusual flours from grains, beans or legumes, such as besan flour from chickpeas. Adjust it to mill anything from a fine flour to coarsely cracked grains.

CAN OPENER Made from solid metal, this heavy-duty attachment holds your can securely in place to open, while a magnet picks up the lid after opening. It can tackle all sizes of tins and if you keep your mixer out on the counter – you can have this as your default attachment.

THE KITCHENAID® BLENDER With its "pulse at any speed" feature, the blender is a worthwhile additional

appliance to complement the KitchenAid stand mixer.

 THE BLENDER uses power and speed to blend, shake, crush, mix and chop its way through smoothies and milkshakes, soups, breadcrumbs, herbs and wonderful crushed ice cocktails. It can produce baby food to just the consistency your child likes it, as well as being a quick way of making up a weekend breakfast pancake batter, a fresh herb salad dressing, an icy sorbet, or a quick sauce for a weeknight pasta. It's so powerful that few jobs take more than 30 seconds, and it can transform a handful of nuts into home-made peanut butter in under a minute.

The KitchenAid blender is a solid, powerful machine — with a stable all-metal base and heavy-duty glass jar. The unique asymmetric and blunt blade powers, rather than splices, its way through ingredients, throwing the food up and around the jar so that it blends together thoroughly, without the mixture catching underneath the blade. The 10-speed touch-button control pad has easy-to-use symbols that take you through from stirring and ice-crushing to liquifying, and the mixing sensor will automatically adjust your speed when it senses more power is needed.

The ultimate ice-crusher, your KitchenAid blender can make fantastic icy fruit drinks and frozen cocktails — crushing hard ice to snow and melting cubes to slush in seconds. Made for professional barmen, the cap for the jar is also a quick measuring jug for small amounts of lime juice and sugar syrup.

PROFESSIONAL TIPS When blending, always start on the slowest speed to prevent splashing and mix everything together thoroughly, then just press the next button when you want to move up to a higher speed.

When making breadcrumbs, process the pieces of bread about five times, for a few seconds each time, at a chop speed ⊙.

When chopping fruits and vegetables, cut into chunks and process a few times on a stir or chop speed ⊛ ⊙ with the pulse button, checking the consistency so as not to overprocess. If you want to take it further to a purée, you'll need to add a little liquid and process at a purée speed ⊛.

When adding extra ingredients while the KitchenAid blender is operating, remove the ingredient cap and add through the top. Keep the machine on one of the two lowest speeds (stir and chop ⊛ ⊙) and stop if the ingredients are hot or the jar is full. When making mayonnaise, it can help to create a small greaseproof cone for the oil to pour slowly down.

Recipe	1	2	3	4	5	6	7	8	9	10	11	12	Country
TZATZIKI p.14	●			●									GREECE
HUMMUS p.14		●				●							LEBANON
GUACAMOLE p.15	●												MEXICO
TARAMASALATA p.15											●		GREECE
TEMPURA p.17	●	●											JAPAN
TOMATO AND ANCHOVY BRUSCHETTA p.18	●			●									ITALY
BLINIS p.18	●	●	●										RUSSIA
TAPENADE CROSTINI p.19	●				●								ITALY
COUNTRY PORK PÂTÉ p.21	●			●	●								INTERNATIONAL
MAYONNAISE p.22		●											FRANCE
AÏOLI p.22		●											FRANCE
CELERIAC REMOULADE p.23		●		●									FRANCE
WHITE CABBAGE AND APPLE SALAD p.24	●			●									GERMANY
RED CABBAGE SALAD p.25	●			●									GERMANY
ICED COURGETTE SOUP WITH SAGE p.26				●							●		FRANCE
PEA SOUP p.28				●	●	●							THE NETHERLANDS
POTATO SOUP p.29				●		●							GERMANY
ONION SOUP GRATINÉE p.29				●									FRANCE
GAZPACHO p.30	●			●									SPAIN
MINESTRONE WITH PESTO p.31				●									ITALY
RED PEPPER AND CHILLI SOUP p.32											●		MEXICO
PIZZA MARGHERITA p.35	●		●										ITALY
BÉCHAMEL SAUCE p.36				●									FRANCE
PESTO p.36				●							●		ITALY
TOMATO PASSATA p.37				●		●							ITALY
BOLOGNESE SAUCE p.37				●	●								ITALY
BASIC PASTA DOUGH p.38	●		●					●					ITALY
LINGUINE WITH GARLIC AND OIL p.40								●					ITALY
TAGLIATELLE WITH PARMESAN AND CORIANDER SAUCE p.41	●		●					●			●		INTERNATIONAL
AUBERGINE AND PARMESAN LASAGNE p.42				●				●					ITALY
PEPPERS AND BROCCOLI LASAGNE p.43				●				●					INTERNATIONAL
CRAB AND SPRING ONION CANNELLONI p.44				●				●					INTERNATIONAL
SPINACH, MUSHROOM AND RICOTTA CANNELLONI p.45	●			●				●					ITALY
RAVIOLI p.46				●	●			●					ITALY
SCHWÄBISCHE MAULTASCHEN p.47	●				●			●					GERMANY
TORTELLINI WITH SMOKED SALMON AND DILL p.48	●			●				●					INTERNATIONAL
SPINACH AND PARMESAN GNOCCHI p.50	●			●									ITALY
FETTUCCINE ALLA ROMANA p.51				●				●					ITALY
SPÄTZLE p.52	●			●									GERMANY
CRAB CAKES WITH MANGO SAMBAL p.55	●	●		●									MALAYSIA
TERRINE OF FISH p.56	●												SPAIN
GEDDE BOLLEN p.57	●				●								NORWAY
LAKSA p.58				●									MALAYSIA
PRAWN AND SPRING ONION CRÊPES p.59	●			●									THAILAND
POACHED SALMON p.60				●									GREAT BRITAIN
CHICKEN, PEPPER AND MUSHROOM PARCELS p.62	●			●									GREAT BRITAIN
TURKEY WITH CHICKPEA PATTIES p.63	●			●									MOROCCO
CHICKEN TANDOORI p.64				●									INDIA
CHICKEN WITH PEPPERS p.65				●									THAILAND
LAMB EN CROÛTE p.66	●												FRANCE
PORK WITH CALVADOS AND APPLES p.68				●									FRANCE
VITELLO TONNATO p.69		●		●	●								ITALY
KJOTTKAKER p.70	●			●	●								NORWAY
FILET AMÉRICAIN WITH BELGIAN FRITES p.72	●				●								BELGIUM
QUICHE LORRAINE p.73	●			●									FRANCE
POLPETTE p.74	●			●	●								ITALY
SWEDISH MEATBALLS p.75	●			●	●								SWEDEN
SPICY SAUSAGES p.76	●				●				●				GERMANY
BRATWURST p.76	●				●				●				GERMANY
BABY CHICKEN WITH CARROTS p.78											●		BABY FOOD
BABY PEACH FOOL p.78											●		BABY FOOD
MASHED POTATOES p.80	●												IRELAND
COLCANNON p.80	●			●									IRELAND
GREEN SAUCE WITH NEW POTATOES p.81	●			●									GERMANY
PISSALADIÈRE p.82			●	●									FRANCE
TORTA PASQUALINA p.84	●		●	●									ITALY
PETITS LÉGUMES FARCIS p.86	●			●	●								FRANCE
CAROTTES VICHY p.87				●									FRANCE
BRAISED RED CABBAGE p.88				●									GERMANY
BRAISED CELERY HEARTS p.88				●									FRANCE
SERVIETTENKNÖDEL p.89		●		●									GERMANY
GRATIN DAUPHINOIS p.90				●									FRANCE

Attachment key (column icons):

Recipe	1	2	3	4	5	6	7	8	9	10	Country
ROSTI WITH APPLE SAUCE p.91				•							GERMANY
SWEET CUCUMBER PICKLE p.92				•							USA
PEACH CHUTNEY p.93				•	•						INDIA
COURGETTE AND TOMATO SAUTE p.94				•							INTERNATIONAL
COURGETTES WITH GARLIC p.94				•							INTERNATIONAL
LEEK AND COURGETTE QUICHE p.95	•			•							FRANCE
SPINACH AND CHEESE SOUFFLE p.96	•	•		•							FRANCE
GRANARY AND WALNUT BREAD p.99	•		•								GREAT BRITAIN
PAIN DE CAMPAGNE p.100			•								FRANCE
TOMATO AND OLIVE BREAD p.101			•								ITALY
PITTA BREAD p.105			•								ISRAEL
SOURDOUGH p.101	•		•								USA
CHALLAH p.105			•								ISRAEL
SODA BREAD p.105	•		•								IRELAND
HUNSRÜCKER BAUERENBROT p.106			•								GERMANY
FOCACCIA p.109			•								ITALY
PRETZELS p.110			•								GERMANY
CHAPATI p.111			•								INDIA
STOLLEN p.112	•		•								GERMANY
PANETTONE p.113			•								ITALY
FLACHSWICKEL p.114			•								GERMANY
LEMON BRIOCHE p.115			•								FRANCE
CROISSANTS p.116	•		•	•							FRANCE
STRUDEL PASTRY p.118			•								GERMANY
FLAKY PASTRY p.118	•										FRANCE
CHOUX PASTRY p.119	•										FRANCE
PÂTE SABLÉE p.119	•										FRANCE
CRÈME PÂTISSIÈRE p.120		•									FRANCE
CRÈME MOUSSELINE p.120	•										FRANCE
CRÈME DESSERT p.121		•									FRANCE
CRÈME ANGLAISE p.121		•									FRANCE
CRÊPES p.122		•									FRANCE
BELGIAN WAFFLES p.123	•	•									BELGIUM
KAISERSCHMARREN p.125	•	•									AUSTRIA
DAMPFKNÖDEL p.126	•		•								GERMANY
OEUFS À LA NEIGE p.127		•									FRANCE
CHOCOLATE MOUSSE p.129		•									FRANCE
GERMKNÖDEL p.129			•								AUSTRIA
TARTE AU CITRON p.130	•	•							•		FRANCE
TARTE AU CHOCOLAT ET À LA FRAMBOISE p.132			•								FRANCE
POTS DE CRÈME AU CHOCOLAT p.133		•									FRANCE
RAISIN CHEESECAKE p.135	•										GERMANY
SCHWARZWÄLDEKIRSCHTORTE p.136		•									GERMANY
KOLDSKAAL p.138		•									DENMARK
KAMMERJUNKER p.138	•										DENMARK
GALETTES À LA FRANGIPANE p.139	•										FRANCE
MERINGUES p.140		•									FRANCE
STRAWBERRY AND PASSION FRUIT PAVLOVA p.141		•									AUSTRALIA
APFEL STRUDEL p.143	•		•	•							GERMANY
TARTE TATIN p.144	•										FRANCE
APPLE PIE p.145	•			•							USA
LEMON AND LIME ICE CREAM p.145		•		•					•		ITALY
MANGO SORBET p.147	•					•					THAILAND
TIRAMISU p.148		•									ITALY
ZABAGLIONE p.148		•									ITALY
RASPBERRY PARFAIT p.149		•			•						FRANCE
FROZEN STRAWBERRY DAIQUIRI p.150										•	INTERNATIONAL
MARGARITA p.150										•	INTERNATIONAL
THE KITCHENAID BIRTHDAY CAKE p.153	•										INTERNATIONAL
GUGELHOPF p.154	•										FRANCE
GÂTEAU SAVOIE p.155		•									FRANCE
MARBLE CAKE p.156	•										GERMANY
TORTA DI MANDORLE p.157		•		•	•						ITALY
APRICOT STREUSEL CAKE p.158	•	•	•								THE NETHERLANDS
PFLAUMENKUCHEN p.159	•										GERMANY
SACHERTORTE p.160		•									AUSTRIA
ORANGE CHIFFON CAKE p.162	•	•							•		USA
WALNUT CAKE WITH SYRUP p.163	•	•			•						GREECE
BUÑUELOS DE MANZANA p.164	•										SPAIN
COCONUT MACAROONS p.165		•									FRANCE
SHORTBREAD p.165	•										GREAT BRITAIN
LEBKUCHEN p.166	•			•							GERMANY
TOPFENKOLATSCHE p.167	•	•	•	•							AUSTRIA
BLUEBERRY MUFFINS p.168	•										USA
SULTANA SCONES p.170	•										GREAT BRITAIN
DOUBLE CHOCOLATE BROWNIES p.171	•			•							USA
SPEKULATIUS p.172		•									AUSTRIA
BISCOTTI p.174	•	•	•								ITALY

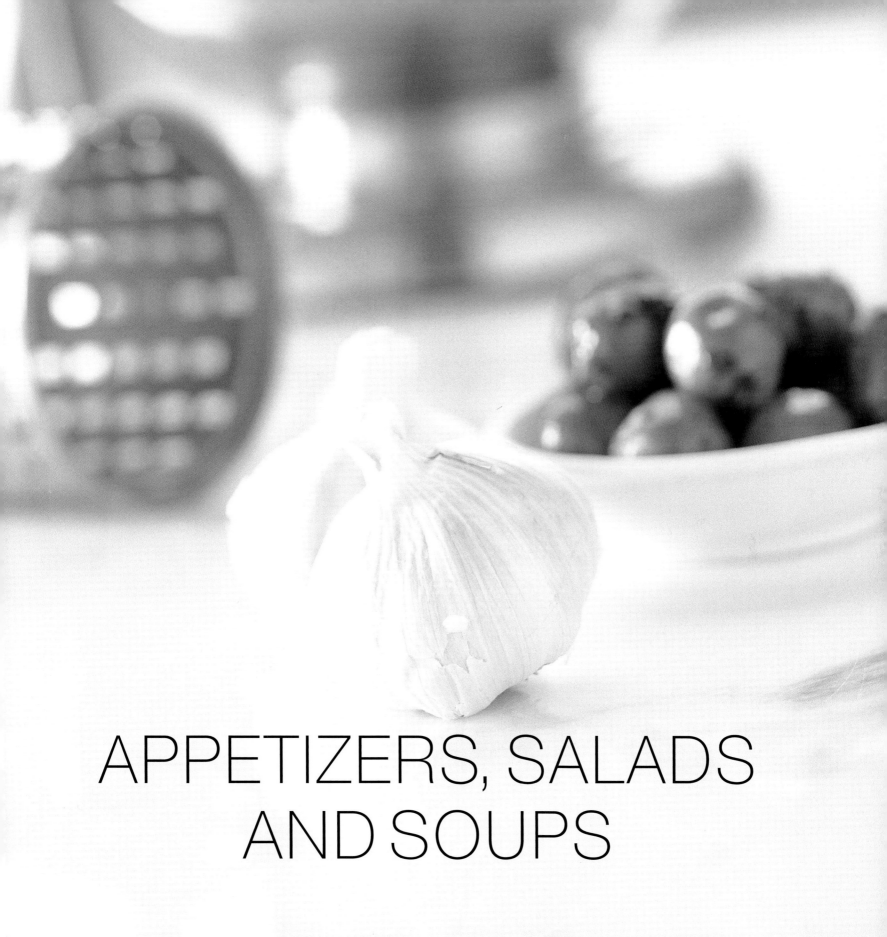

APPETIZERS, SALADS AND SOUPS

TZATZIKI Although the Greek dip tzatziki is usually served

simply as a snack or a starter with bread, it is also a delicious accompaniment

to grilled lamb chops or baked or grilled fish.

HUMMUS A Middle-Eastern dish made from puréed

chickpeas and tahini, a sesame seed paste, and served as a dip with

pitta bread or with kebabs.

SERVES 6

Preparation time: 25 minutes plus
10 minutes chilling time

Attachments used

2 small cucumbers or 1 large firm cucumber (about 400 g), unpeeled

1 tsp salt

600 g Greek yoghurt

2–3 cloves garlic, crushed

1 Tbsp white wine vinegar

2 Tbsp extra-virgin olive oil

Freshly ground black pepper

Few fresh mint leaves

1 With the coarse shredding drum on the rotary slicer/shredder, on speed 4, shred the cucumber into a bowl, sprinkle with the salt and leave for 10 minutes. Pour off any excess liquid, then place the cucumber into a sieve and gently squeeze out any remaining water.

2 Transfer the cucumber to the mixer bowl and, using the flat beater, stir in the yoghurt. Add the crushed garlic to the cucumber together with the vinegar and olive oil. Stir well, then add seasoning to taste and chill in the refrigerator for 10 minutes. Serve chilled with the mint leaves on top.

SERVES 8

Preparation time: 10 minutes

Attachments used

600 g canned chickpeas, drained

50 ml/¼ cup cold water

50 ml/¼ cup fresh lemon juice

50 g tahini

3 cloves garlic, crushed

½ tsp salt

¼ tsp paprika (optional)

1 Using the strainer, on speed 4, strain the chickpeas into the mixer bowl. Return the waste to the strained chickpeas.

2 Add the water, lemon juice, tahini, garlic, salt, and paprika, if using. Using the wire whip, on speed 4, whisk for 1 minute. Stop and scrape the ingredients back down into the bowl. Increase to speed 10 and whisk for 1 minute, or until smooth. Serve with toasted pitta bread.

GUACAMOLE An irresistible dip to enjoy with a

glass of something cool on a summer's evening, this famous fiery avocado

dip originates from Mexico.

TARAMASALATA This Greek meze dip is made

from tarama, salted coral-pink fish roe, originally taken from the grey mullet

but now more usually cod.

SERVES 4 TO 6

Preparation time: 15 minutes

Attachments used

2 large ripe avocados, cut in half and stoned

1 clove garlic

6 spring onions, finely chopped

2 tomatoes, skinned, deseeded and chopped

1 small green chilli, finely chopped (optional)

1 Tbsp chopped fresh coriander

Juice of 1 lime

Salt and freshly ground black pepper

1 Using a teaspoon, scrape the avocado flesh into the mixer bowl. Using the flat beater on speed 2, beat the avocado to a smooth purée.

2 Crush the garlic to a paste with a little salt and add to the mixer bowl with all the other ingredients. Beat again until well mixed. Chill until required.

SERVES 4 TO 6

Preparation time: 30 minutes plus

1 hour chilling time

Blender used

4–5 slices (about 200 g) 2-day-old white bread, crusts discarded

4 Tbsp warm water

100–125 g tarama

3 Tbsp olive oil

3–4 Tbsp lemon juice

Salt and freshly ground black pepper

1 Tear the bread into pieces, place in a bowl and pour over the warm water. Leave for 10 minutes, then squeeze out any excess water and place into the blender. Blend briefly on mix speed . Add the tarama and blend, still on mix speed, until a paste is formed.

2 With the motor running, gradually add the olive oil and the lemon juice until a smooth purée is formed. Scrape into a bowl and add seasoning to taste, taking care not to add too much salt. Cover and chill in the refrigerator for 1 hour. When ready to serve, stir the taramasalata and spoon onto a plate. Serve with pitta bread

TEMPURA
A Japanese dish where a light batter is used to coat pieces of seafood, meat or vegetables, then deep-fried until it puffs up. It is served with a special dipping sauce made from soy and white wine vinegar.

SERVES 4

Preparation time: 1 hour

Cooking time: 30 minutes

Attachments used

225 g large prawns, peeled but tails left intact

175-g piece middle-cut salmon fillet

1 red pepper, deseeded

1 yellow pepper, deseeded

1 large or 2 small courgettes

For the dipping sauce

2 Tbsp light soy sauce

1 Tbsp rice wine vinegar or white wine vinegar

1 Tbsp sweet chilli sauce

Sliced fresh red chilli, to garnish

For the batter

1 large egg, separated

350 ml/1^1/$_2$ cups ice-cold water

100 g plain flour

Salt

Sunflower oil, for deep-frying

1 Remove the thin black vein that runs down the back of each prawn, rinse well and dry on kitchen paper. Discard the skin and any bones from the salmon and cut into bite-sized cubes, rinse and pat dry. Cut the peppers into thin strips, then cut the courgettes into strips. Blend all the dipping sauce ingredients together.

2 To make the batter, place the egg yolk in the mixer bowl and gradually pour the ice-cold water onto the egg yolk. Sieve the flour then tip into the bowl with the salt. Using the flat beater, on speed 1, mix for 1 minute or until just incorporated. Pour into a large bowl.

3 Clean the mixer bowl and dry thoroughly, then using the wire whip, on speed 10, whisk the egg white until very soft peaks are formed. Gently fold the egg white into the batter.

In recipes where you need to fold whisked egg whites into a mixture that you have prepared with the flat beater, it is very useful to own a second mixer bowl so you can whip the egg whites without having to first transfer the mixture, and clean and dry the bowl.

4 Heat the oil to 190°C in a wok or a deep-fat fryer and have ready a plate or tray lined with plenty of kitchen paper. Dip a few pieces of the seafood into the prepared batter, until lightly coated, allowing any excess to drip back into the bowl. Fry in the hot oil for 2 to 3 minutes or until thoroughly cooked. Remove from the oil and drain well on the kitchen paper.

5 When all the seafood is cooked, coat the vegetables in the remaining batter, and fry for 1 to 2 minutes. Drain well. Serve the tempura with the dipping sauce.

TOMATO AND ANCHOVY BRUSCHETTA
Tuscan toasted bread, brushed with garlic and topped with fresh tomatoes. For a more garlicky flavour, you could crush the garlic over the bread before spreading on the tomatoes.

SERVES 6

Preparation time: 8 minutes

Cooking time: 2 minutes

Attachments used

6 medium firm plum tomatoes, deseeded

2 anchovy fillets, drained

2 Tbsp extra-virgin olive oil

Salt and freshly ground black pepper

6 cloves garlic

6 thick slices baguette, or crusty bread, toasted

1 Use the rotary slicer/shredder, fitted with the medium shredding drum, and mince the tomatoes and anchovies, on speed 4, into the mixer bowl.

2 With the flat beater on speed 4, gradually add the olive oil and then season with the salt and freshly ground black pepper.

3 Cut the garlic cloves in half and rub the cut ends over one side of each bread slice. Spread the tomato paste on top of the bread, then cook under a preheated grill for 1 to 2 minutes or until warm. Serve immediately.

BLINIS
Little Russian pancakes made from buckwheat flour that have become synonymous with cocktails and caviar. Alternative toppings include a spoon of sour cream with some chives, smoked salmon or salmon roe.

SERVES 6

Preparation time: 40 minutes plus

1 hour 30 minutes standing time

Cooking time: 35 minutes

Attachments used

250 ml/1 cup milk

150 g buckwheat flour

1 packet (7 g) active dry yeast

200 g plain flour

1 egg, separated

10 g salt

250 g crème fraîche

1 Warm the milk in a small saucepan to just below boiling point. Put the buckwheat flour and yeast in the mixer bowl. Using the dough hook, on speed 4, add half of the milk to the flour mixture until well combined. Cover and leave to stand at room temperature for 1 hour until the mixture has doubled in volume.

2 Add the plain flour, egg yolk, salt, crème fraîche and the remaining milk to the bowl. Change to the flat beater and mix well on speed 4 until the mixture is smooth. Allow the mixture to stand for a further 30 minutes. Transfer to another bowl.

3 Clean the mixer bowl and dry thoroughly, then whisk the egg whites using the wire whip on speed 8 until peaking. Fold the egg whites into the batter carefully.

4 Heat two blini pans or one heavy-based frying pan over a low heat for 7 minutes before using. Lightly grease the pans and spoon in enough batter to make a blini of 5-mm thickness. Cook over a gentle heat for 2 to 3 minutes until browned on the underside, flip the blini over and cook for a further minute. Remove from the pan and keep the blinis warm while repeating the cooking process with the remaining batter. Serve hot.

TAPENADE CROSTINI
Another Tuscan speciality, these thin slices of toast are topped with an olive paste made with anchovies and capers. Crostini can also be served with chicken livers, peppers or aubergines.

SERVES 4 TO 6

Preparation time: 5 minutes

250 g black olives, stoned

50-g can anchovy fillets, drained thoroughly

1 Tbsp capers

2 cloves garlic

2 Tbsp shredded fresh basil

About 200 ml/¾ cup extra-virgin olive oil

1 large ciabatta loaf, sliced

2 Tbsp shredded fresh basil, to garnish

Attachments used

1 Using the food grinder fitted with the fine grinding plate, on speed 4, mince the black olives, anchovy fillets, capers and garlic into the mixer bowl and add 2 tablespoons shredded basil leaves.

2 With the flat beater on speed 4, gradually pour in just enough olive oil for the mixture to come together and form a spreadable consistency. Scrape into a bowl, cover lightly and store in the refrigerator until required.

3 Lightly toast the bread on both sides until crisp, top with the black olive paste, scatter over a few shredded basil leaves and serve immediately.

COUNTRY PORK PÂTÉ
The olives in this country-style pâté could be replaced with mushrooms, while chorizo or salami can be added for extra flavour. The pâté can be frozen for up to a month.

SERVES 6 TO 8

Preparation time: 20 minutes,
          plus 1 to 2 days chilling

Cooking time: 2 hours

Attachments used

3 shallots

2–4 cloves garlic

2 Tbsp butter

450-g piece pork belly, rind and bones removed

175 g veal or pork fillet

175 g chicken livers

150-g piece prosciutto or pancetta

125 g stoned black olives

5 Tbsp chopped fresh mixed herbs (thyme, parsley, basil)

2–3 Tbsp brandy

Salt and freshly ground black pepper

8–10 rashers rindless back bacon

1   Preheat the oven to 160°C/Gas Mark 3. Using the rotary slicer/shredder, with the medium shredding drum attached, on speed 4, chop the shallots and garlic. Heat the butter in a frying pan and sauté the shallot mixture for 5 minutes or until softened. Leave until cool.

2   Change to the food grinder and, with the fine grinding plate, on speed 4, mince the belly of pork, veal or pork fillet, the chicken livers and prosciutto into a bowl. Chop the olives roughly. Add the remaining ingredients, except for the bacon, and mix together using the flat beater.

3   Line a 1.1-litre terrine dish with the bacon, leaving the ends so that they hang over the sides. Place the meat mixture into the dish and pack down firmly. Fold the bacon over the top and cover with either a lid or a double sheet of aluminium foil.

4   Place in a roasting tin half-filled with hot water. Cook in the oven for 1 hour 45 minutes to 2 hours or until the pâté has begun to shrink away from the sides of the dish and a skewer inserted into the centre comes out clean.

The easiest way to mince raw meat or fish is to chill or partially freeze it to prevent any getting caught in the food grinder. Cutting away gristle and sinew also stops the meat becoming entangled in the knife or grinding plate.

5   Remove from the roasting tin and leave to cool for about an hour. Uncover the terrine dish, cover with clean foil and weigh down with either clean weights or cans. Leave to cool completely, then place in the refrigerator.

6   Store the pâté in the refrigerator for 1 to 2 days before serving, keeping the weights in place, then eat within 2 to 3 days. Before serving, take the pâté out to return to room temperature for 30 minutes.

MAYONNAISE

One of the most versatile of French sauces, mayonnaise can be used as a summer dressing for vegetables and eggs, with fresh seafood, meats or for dipping fries. This version is made with a whole egg and is very easy to do.

MAKES 200 ML/1 CUP

Preparation time: 15 minutes

1 large egg

1 egg yolk

1 tsp white wine vinegar or lemon juice

1 tsp Dijon mustard

200 ml/1 cup olive oil

Salt and freshly ground black pepper

Attachments used

1 Warm the mixer bowl and wire whip with hot water, then dry thoroughly. Make sure all the ingredients are at room temperature.

2 Place the egg, egg yolk, vinegar or lemon juice and mustard in the mixer bowl, attach the wire whip and whisk, at speed 10, until well combined and frothy.

3 Add the oil very gradually, drop by drop at first, then more steadily as the mixture starts to thicken.

4 When all the oil has been absorbed, season with the salt and black pepper and add extra vinegar or lemon juice if required. The mixture should be very thick and stiff.

AÏOLI

A summery Provençal dish of garlic mayonnaise, which is usually eaten with fresh vegetables, but can also be served with a salad, eggs, poached fish or a cold chicken. By leaving out the garlic, you can also use this recipe to make a rich, yolk-only mayonnaise.

MAKES 600 ML/2¹/₂ CUPS

Preparation time: 10 minutes

5 cloves garlic

Pinch of salt

3 egg yolks

450 ml/2 cups olive oil

1 Tbsp lemon juice

Attachments used

1 Finely chop the garlic and put into a pestle and mortar with the salt. Pound until smooth.

2 Warm the mixer bowl and wire whip with hot water, then dry thoroughly. Make sure all the ingredients are at room temperature.

3 Place the egg yolks and garlic in the mixer bowl and, with the wire whip, whisk on speed 6 for 1 minute until creamy.

4 Reducing the speed to speed 4, very slowly add the oil, drop by drop at first, ensuring each addition is fully incorporated before adding more, then gradually begin to add in a slow stream once the mixture is glossy and starts to thicken.

5 When all the oil has been absorbed, add the lemon juice if the mixture seems too thick.

CELERIAC REMOULADE
This classic French dish is made from the winter root vegetable celeriac, a type of celery that can be eaten raw or cooked, but is most famously used in this creamy salad.

SERVES 4
Preparation time: 20 minutes

Attachments used

1 Tbsp mustard
5 Tbsp vegetable oil
Juice of 1 lemon
1 Tbsp vinegar
1 Tbsp crème fraîche
Salt and freshly ground black pepper
450 g celeriac
Small lettuce leaves, to garnish

1 Place the mustard, oil and lemon juice in the mixer bowl and, using the wire whip, whisk together on speed 10. Add the vinegar and crème fraîche, season, then mix together again.

2 Peel the celeriac with a sharp knife and chop it into pieces. Using the rotary slicer/shredder, fitted with the medium shredding drum, on speed 4, grate the celeriac and toss it in the sauce immediately, to prevent it discolouring. Garnish the remoulade with lettuce leaves and serve.

WHITE CABBAGE AND APPLE SALAD
A creamy German cabbage salad that marinates in a sour cream and white wine vinegar dressing overnight to produce a delicious salad that can be served with cheese and bread or sausage.

SERVES 6

Preparation time: 10 minutes plus overnight standing time

Attachments used

1 small white cabbage
1–2 shallots, peeled
3 small eating apples, peeled and cored
Salt and freshly ground black pepper
1 Tbsp white wine vinegar
4 Tbsp sour cream
2 Tbsp walnut halves

1 Remove the outer leaves and hard inner core of the cabbage and cut into wedges. Cut the shallots in half.

2 Using the rotary slicer/shreder, with the coarse shredding drum attached, on speed 4, shred the cabbage, shallots and apples into the mixer bowl. Add seasoning to taste and, using the flat beater, stir until well mixed.

3 Blend the vinegar and sour cream together and pour over the cabbage, mix well, cover and store in the refrigerator overnight.

4 When ready to serve, use the rotary slicer/shredder, with the coarse shredding drum attached, on speed 4, to chop the walnuts. Spoon the cabbage salad into a serving bowl and sprinkle with the nuts.

RED CABBAGE SALAD
This attractive German red cabbage salad goes well with both hot and cold foods.

To turn it into a light lunch dish, chop and add some cooked bratwurst sausage or ham.

SERVES 6

Preparation time: 15 minutes

Attachments used

¹/₂ small red cabbage (about 450 g)

2 carrots, peeled

1 white onion

2 green eating apples

2 Tbsp lemon juice

75 g baby corn, halved lengthways

50 g dried cranberries (optional)

For the dressing

4 Tbsp sour cream

1 tsp German or English mustard

1 tsp sugar

2 Tbsp white wine vinegar

Salt and freshly ground black pepper

¹/₂–1 tsp caraway seeds

1 Remove the outer leaves and hard central core from the cabbage. With the slicing drum on the rotary slicer/shredder, on speed 4, slice the red cabbage into a colander. Rinse well under cold water until the water runs clear. Drain thoroughly then place in the mixer bowl.

2 With the coarse shredding drum on the rotary slicer/shredder, on speed 4, shred the carrots and the onion into the mixer bowl.

3 Core the apple, peel if preferred, then coarsely shred, on speed 4, into a small bowl. Add the lemon juice and toss well, then stir into the red cabbage mixture.

4 Blanch the baby corn in a pan of salted boiling water for 3 minutes, drain and add to the cabbage, together with the dried cranberries, if using. Mix lightly together.

5 To make the dressing, place all the ingredients in the mixer bowl and, using the flat beater on speed 2, blend together, then pour over the cabbage. Toss everything lightly together and serve.

ICED COURGETTE SOUP WITH SAGE This chilled summer soup makes a beautiful starter

or a light lunch. You could replace the Parmesan with old Edam cheese and use nut oil instead of olive oil.

SERVES 4

Preparation time: 10 minutes

Cooking time: 10 minutes

2 courgettes

50 g Parmesan cheese

2 Tbsp olive oil

2 ice cubes

Salt and freshly ground black pepper

16 sage leaves

1$^{1}/_{2}$ Tbsp oil, for frying

Cayenne pepper (optional)

Attachments used

Blender used

1 Attach the slicing drum to the rotary slicer/shredder and slice the courgettes. Cook in a pan of salted boiling water for 5 minutes. Drain the slices and leave to cool. Shave the Parmesan into thin slices.

2 In the blender, mix the courgettes on stir speed with the olive oil, ice cubes, four pinches of salt and freshly ground black pepper until liquified.

3 Rinse and pat dry the sage leaves. Heat the remaining oil in a frying pan, add the leaves and fry for 1 minute, then drain them on kitchen paper. Keep four leaves aside.

4 Chop the other 12 sage leaves and stir into the courgette mixture. Pour into four bowls. Garnish each with a sage leaf and some Parmesan flakes, and dust with cayenne pepper if desired.

PEA SOUP
Pea soups are a favourite wintertime dish in Holland and Belgium and this one is a meal in itself, with croûtons of bread, golden fried onions and crispy bacon pieces added just before serving.

SERVES 4 TO 6

Preparation time: 20 minutes

Cooking time: 20 minutes

Attachments used

850 g frozen peas, thawed

1.2 litres chicken or vegetable stock

Salt and freshly ground black pepper

1 tsp dried marjoram

2 Tbsp chopped fresh parsley

4 Tbsp single cream (optional)

200 g back bacon rashers

1 large onion

40 g butter

5 slices white bread

1 Using the food grinder fitted with the fine grinding plate, on speed 4, mince the peas. Place in a saucepan, add the stock, bring to the boil, then add a little seasoning with the dried marjoram. Cover with a lid, reduce the heat and simmer for 15 minutes or until really soft.

2 Pass the peas with their liquid through the strainer, on speed 4, return to the rinsed pan, adjust the seasoning and add the chopped parsley. Heat through until hot and keep warm. Just before serving, stir in the cream.

3 Meanwhile attach the rotary slicer/shredder with the coarse shredding drum attached, on speed 4, and pass the bacon through and then the onion separately.

4 Heat half of the butter and sauté the bacon until crisp, remove with a slotted draining spoon and reserve. Add the onion to the butter remaining in the pan and fry until softened. Drain well.

5 Discard the crusts from the bread and cut into small cubes. Heat the remaining butter in a frying pan and sauté the cubes for 5 minutes, stirring frequently, or until crisp and golden.

6 Mix the bacon, onion and croûtons together and serve with the soup.

POTATO SOUP

Hearty country-style potato soups are a mainstay of the European winter. This version is made with celery, carrot and leek and can be garnished with bacon, croûtons and spring onions or a swirl of sour cream and chives.

SERVES 4

Preparation time: 15 minutes

Cooking time: 45 minutes

Attachments used

1 kg potatoes, cut into wedges

4 celery sticks

1 carrot

1 leek, trimmed and washed well

1 onion, sliced

100 g butter

250 ml/1^1/$_4$ cups water

Salt and freshly ground black pepper

250 ml/1^1/$_4$ cups cream or crème fraîche

^{1}/$_4$ tsp freshly grated nutmeg, or to taste

Croûtons, to garnish

Crispy fried chopped bacon, to garnish

Diagonally sliced spring onions, to garnish

1 Using the rotary slicer/shredder, with the slicing drum attached, on speed 4, slice the potatoes into the mixer bowl, then remove them to a large saucepan. Still on speed 4, slice the celery, carrot, leek and onion separately.

2 Add 50 g of the butter to the saucepan and place over a gentle heat. Cook gently, stirring frequently until the potatoes are coated in the butter. Add the celery and carrot and cook for a further 2 minutes, stirring.

3 Pour in the water, add seasoning and bring to the boil. Cover and simmer for 20 to 25 minutes, or until the potatoes are really tender.

4 Attach the strainer and, on speed 4, pass half the soup through the strainer and return to a clean saucepan. Stir in the remaining unpuréed soup.

5 Melt the remaining butter, and sauté the leek and onion for 5 to 8 minutes or until softened, then stir the leek mixture, together with any butter remaining in the pan, into the soup. Stir in the cream or crème fraîche with the nutmeg and heat gently, stirring and taking care not to allow the soup to boil. Adjust the seasoning and serve garnished with croûtons, crispy bacon and sliced spring onions.

ONION SOUP GRATINÉE

This version of the French bistro classic is made with coarsely sliced onions, cooked slowly, then heated under the grill to let the Gruyère melt over the toasted bread and soup.

SERVES 4

Preparation time: 40 minutes

Cooking time: 10 minutes

Attachments used

110 g Gruyère cheese

400 g onions

4 large slices baguette

1 Tbsp butter

1 Tbsp plain flour

1.2 litres/5 cups warm water

Salt and freshly ground black pepper

2 tsp fresh chives

1 Using the rotary slicer/shredder with the medium shredding drum attached, on speed 4, grate the cheese. Change to the slicing drum and slice the onions, on speed 4. Toast the bread in an oven or in a frying pan.

2 In a casserole, sauté the sliced onions in the butter over a low heat, stirring occasionally, for about 25 minutes. Dust the onions with the flour and continue to sauté until golden brown, stirring constantly. Add the warm water, mix well and leave to cook for 10 minutes.

3 Add three-quarters of the cheese to the casserole. Season with salt and pepper and stir in the chives.

4 Pour the soup into individual soup bowls or a large tureen. Top with the toasted slices of bread and sprinkle with the remaining cheese. Place briefly under a preheated grill to melt the cheese, then serve immediately.

GAZPACHO
A classic summer soup from Spain that tastes best when made with ripe and flavourful Mediterranean tomatoes and vegetables and Spanish olive oil. Add the ice cubes and serve it very cold.

SERVES 4 TO 6

Preparation time: 15 minutes plus at least 1 hour chilling time

Attachments used

750 g ripe tomatoes, cores removed
1 red pepper, deseeded
1 green pepper, deseeded
1 red onion
½ cucumber, deseeded
2 cloves garlic, finely chopped
1 Tbsp finely chopped fresh parsley
1 Tbsp finely chopped fresh basil leaves
1½ Tbsp red wine vinegar
125 ml/½ cup passata
80 ml/⅓ cup water
3 drops Tabasco
4 Tbsp olive oil
Salt and freshly ground black pepper
Cubes of frozen olive oil and fresh basil leaves, to serve

1 Using the rotary slicer/shredder with the slicing drum attached, on speed 4, coarsely grate all the vegetables into the mixer bowl.

2 Add all the other ingredients and mix thoroughly with the flat beater on speed 4, seasoning well with salt and pepper. Refrigerate for 12 hours if possible, to allow the flavours to mellow and blend

3 Serve this soup with cubes of frozen olive oil and some fresh basil leaves

MINESTRONE WITH PESTO
A thick Italian vegetable soup, which can be served as a whole meal with some bread. The borlotti beans in the recipe can be replaced with either haricot or kidney beans.

SERVES 4 TO 6

Preparation time: 20 minutes plus overnight soaking if using dried beans

Cooking time: 1 hour

Attachments used

200 g dried borlotti beans or 400 g canned borlotti beans, rinsed and drained

4 small potatoes, peeled

2 carrots

2 small leeks

2 celery stalks

2 small courgettes

1 onion

1.5 litres water

4 Tbsp olive oil, plus extra to serve

2 medium tomatoes, skinned, deseeded and roughly chopped

50 g borage sprigs (preferably with flowers)

150 g shortcut macaroni

2 Tbsp pesto (see page 36)

Salt and freshly ground black pepper

Freshly grated Parmesan cheese, to serve

1 If using dried beans, rinse them well, then cover with plenty of cold water and leave overnight. Drain well, then place the beans in a saucepan and cover with water. Bring to the boil, then drain and cover again with cold water. Return to the boil and simmer for 15 minutes, then drain and reserve.

2 Using the rotary slicer/shredder, fitted with the slicing drum, on speed 4, slice all the vegetables, except the tomatoes, into the mixer bowl.

3 Bring the water to the boil, add the beans – if using dried – and the prepared vegetables. Stir in the olive oil, return to the boil, then cover the pan and simmer for 30 minutes.

4 Add the tomatoes and the borage leaves to the soup, together with the canned beans if using. Cook for a further 15 minutes.

5 About 5 minutes before the end of the cooking time, add the pasta to the soup. Cook until firm to the bite, *al dente*.

6 Mix the pesto with a ladleful of the hot soup, then stir into the rest of the soup with seasoning to taste. Serve immediately, with extra olive oil and black pepper, and sprinkled with the Parmesan cheese. Decorate with borage flowers if available.

RED PEPPER AND CHILLI SOUP

For a dramatic effect, make two batches of this Mexican-style soup, using red peppers in one and yellow peppers in the other. To serve, ladle the red pepper soup into shallow soup bowls, then ladle some of the yellow pepper into the centre to form a 'sunburst'.

SERVES 4

Preparation time: 15 minutes

Cooking time: 30 minutes

Blender used

2 Tbsp olive oil

1 onion, roughly chopped

1–3 cloves garlic, sliced

1 red chilli, deseeded and chopped

4 red peppers, skinned, deseeded and sliced

3 tomatoes, skinned and deseeded

900 ml/3³/4 cups vegetable or chicken stock

Salt and freshly ground black pepper

Sour cream and snipped fresh chives, to garnish

1 Heat the oil in a large pan and sauté the onion, garlic and chilli for 5 minutes, stirring frequently. Add the peppers and continue to sauté for a further 2 minutes. Stir in the tomatoes together with the stock and a little seasoning and bring to the boil.

2 Cover with a lid, reduce the heat and simmer for 20 minutes, or until the peppers are really soft. Remove from the heat and allow to cool. Place in the blender and mix on purée speed 🌀 until the mixture is well combined. If you want a really smooth soup, rub the purée through a fine sieve. Return the soup to the pan, adjust the seasoning and reheat gently.

3 Pour into warmed soup bowls. Swirl the soup with sour cream and sprinkle with the chives. Serve with fresh bread.

PIZZA, PASTA, GNOCCHI AND NOODLES

PIZZA MARGHERITA
One of Italy's original pizzas, created in Naples to honour the visiting Queen Margherita. This recipe makes enough for two pizzas - if you only want to make one, freeze one portion of the dough and cut the topping ingredients in half.

MAKES 2 PIZZAS

Preparation time: 10 minutes plus standing time

Cooking time: 15 to 20 minutes

Attachments used

375 g strong white bread flour

$1/2$ tsp salt

1 packet (7 g) active dry yeast

2 Tbsp olive oil

250 ml/$1^{1}/_{3}$ cups tepid water

For the toppings

Two 400-g cans chopped or whole tomatoes, mashed and drained

300 g mozzarella cheese, thinly sliced.

Olive oil

Salt

Two handfuls of fresh basil

1 Preheat the oven to 220°C/Gas Mark 7. Place the flour, salt and yeast into the mixer bowl. Using the flat beater, on speed 2, mix the dry ingredients together for a few seconds.

2 Change to the dough hook and, on speed 2, add the olive oil, then gradually add the water and begin to knead. If the dough looks at all dry, add a little more water until the mixture looks moist. Knead for about 1 minute only on this speed.

3 Cover with the plastic bowl cover and leave to rise in a warm, draught-free place for about 1 hour, or until doubled in bulk.

4 Knead well again, adding a little extra flour if the dough seems too sticky. The machine may be stopped once or twice and the dough pulled away from hook.

5 Divide the dough in two and roll out into thin circles. Grease two baking sheets.

6 Put the tomatoes on first with your fingers or a fork, trying not to make the dough too wet. Add the slices of mozzarella, then a drizzle of olive oil, some salt and the basil. Bake in the oven for 15 to 20 minutes until golden.

VARIATIONS

MUSHROOM AND PARMA HAM PIZZA – Sauté a chopped onion, 2–3 crushed cloves garlic and 225 g assorted sliced mushrooms for 5 minutes, then add a 400-g can chopped tomatoes and simmer for another 5 minutes. Drain thoroughly and spread over one of the pizza bases. Top with 100 g Parma ham strips and 100 g sliced mozzarella. Bake, then serve sprinkled with some shredded basil.

SPINACH AND GOAT'S CHEESE PIZZA – Sauté a chopped onion and 2-3 crushed cloves garlic for 3 minutes. Add a deseeded and sliced yellow pepper and 2 sliced tomatoes to the pan and cook for a further 3 minutes. Drain thoroughly, then mix with 225 g thawed and well drained frozen spinach, $1/4$ tsp freshly grated nutmeg and some seasoning. Spread this mixture over one of the pizza bases and top with 1 Tbsp chopped fresh oregano and 225 g crumbled goat's cheese before baking.

PASTA SAUCES

These are the four classic Italian sauces, which can be used to make lasagnes or cannelloni. They are all wonderful on their own, served with home-made pasta. The béchamel sauce can also be used in place of a simple roux.

BÉCHAMEL SAUCE

This French white sauce is flavoured with vegetables and can be used as a topping for lasagne or cannelloni or to bind together a pasta sauce or vegetable gratin.

MAKES 300 ML/1¼ CUPS

Preparation time: 10 minutes plus 15 minutes infusing time
Cooking time: 10 minutes

Attachments used

1 small onion, cut into wedges
1 small carrot, cut into chunks
1 celery stick
1 bay leaf
300 ml/1¼ cups milk
1 blade mace
40 g butter
40 g plain flour
Salt and freshly ground black pepper
1–2 Tbsp single cream (optional)

1 Using the rotary slicer/shredder, with the slicing drum attached, on speed 4, slice the vegetables into the mixer bowl, then place them in a heavy-based saucepan. Add the bay leaf and the milk with the mace.

2 Place over a gentle heat and warm until almost at boiling point, then remove, cover with a lid and leave to infuse for 15 minutes, or longer if time permits. Strain and discard the vegetables and herbs.

3 Melt the butter in a heavy-based saucepan, then sprinkle in the flour and cook over a gentle heat for 2 minutes, stirring throughout. Draw off the heat, then gradually stir in the strained milk.

4 Return to the heat and cook, stirring, until the sauce thickens and coats the back of a wooden spoon. Remove from the heat and add seasoning to taste and the cream if using.

PESTO

This fresh Italian sauce from Genoa makes a great marinade for grilled chicken or fish, or it can be stirred into home-made pasta; a spoonful added to a bowl of vegetable soup; or drizzled over a mozzarella and tomato salad.

MAKES 170 ML/¾ CUP

Preparation time: 15 minutes

Attachments used
Blender used

50 g Parmesan or Pecorino cheese
25 g fresh basil leaves
50 g toasted pine kernels
150 ml/⅔ cup extra-virgin olive oil
Freshly ground black pepper

1 Using a grater, or attaching the fine shredding drum to the rotary slicer/shredder, on speed 4, grate the Parmesan cheese.

2 Place the basil leaves and pine kernels in the blender and blend at stir speed until finely chopped. Then, with the motor running, slowly pour in the olive oil, drop by drop. When about half the oil has been added, you can gradually start to add bigger amounts of oil, until it has all been used.

3 Scrape the mixture into a bowl, stir in the grated Parmesan and season to taste with the pepper. Store any excess, covered, in the refrigerator.

TOMATO PASSATA
This basic Italian cooked tomato passata can be eaten on its own with pasta, a little basil and Parmesan or added to pasta sauces, stews or used on pizza bases. Try to pick very ripe tomatoes with lots of flavour.

SERVES 4

Preparation time: 5 minutes

Cooking time: 45 minutes

1 kg fresh tomatoes, quartered

1 onion

1 stick celery

1 carrot

2 Tbsp olive oil

Salt and freshly ground black pepper

Attachments used

1 Using the strainer, on speed 4, process the tomatoes into a saucepan.

2 Attach the fine shredding drum and shred the onion, celery and carrot. Heat the oil and saute the grated vegetables until soft. Add to the saucepan with the tomatoes. Season and bring to the boill. Simmer for 40 minutes until a thick sauce is obtained.

BOLOGNESE SAUCE
An authentic Italian Bolognese sauce, made with your own minced steak and pork to ensure that the meat is very tender. Spinach tagliatelle also goes really well with this.

SERVES 4

Preparation time: 30 minutes

Cooking time: 40 minutes

1 celery stalk, trimmed

1 onion

1 large carrot

300 g lean beef (topside, sirloin or blade)

80 g pork

1 Tbsp butter or olive oil

6 medium ripe tomatoes, peeled and chopped

1 Tbsp tomato purée

200 ml/^{2}/$_3$ cup beef stock

Salt and freshly ground black pepper

1 bay leaf (optional)

Freshly grated Parmesan cheese

Attachments used

1 Cut the vegetables into chunks and using the food grinder, fitted with the coarse grinding plate, on speed 4, mince into the mixer bowl. Cut the beef and pork into strips and feed through the food grinder into the bowl.

2 Heat the butter or oil in a large saucepan and sauté the vegetables and meat for 5 to 8 minutes, stirring frequently until the meat is browned.

3 Cook for 2 minutes, then add the tomatoes and tomato purée and gradually stir in the stock. Add seasoning to taste, and the bay leaf if using, and bring to the boil. Cover with a lid, reduce the heat and simmer for 30 minutes. Adjust the seasoning and serve with tagliatelle and Parmesan cheese.

BASIC PASTA DOUGH

This pasta dough recipe can be used to make any of the recipes in this book. Simply cut the rolled out dough into sheets for lasagne and ravioli, or pass through the cutters to make tagliatelle or linguine.

MAKES 450 g PASTA DOUGH

Preparation time: 10 minutes plus 1 hour chilling time

Attachments used

300 g 00 flour, durum wheat flour or plain flour
3 medium eggs
1 Tbsp olive oil

1 Place the flour, eggs and oil in the mixer bowl and attach the flat beater. On speed 1, mix slowly until the mixture is thoroughly incorporated. Exchange the flat beater for the dough hook and gradually increase the speed to 4, kneading for 5 to 8 minutes until a smooth, elastic pasta dough is formed. Wrap in clingfilm and leave to chill in the refrigerator for at least 1 hour.

2 Attach the pasta roller to the mixer and set the adjustment knob to 1. Cut the dough into eight pieces and pass one portion very slowly through the roller at speed 2, then fold it in half. Do this four to five times. When the dough is no longer sticky, set the adjustment knob to 2 and pass the pasta through, but do not fold the dough this time. Continue rolling the dough through four to five times on each setting until the desired setting is reached. Repeat with the other portions of dough. The pasta dough is now ready to be cut.

VARIATIONS

SPINACH PASTA – Instead of one of the eggs, add 50 g cooked, very well-drained and chopped spinach to the mixer bowl.

BLACK INK PASTA – Add 1 teaspoon of squid ink to the mixer bowl with the rest of the ingredients.

RED BEET PASTA – In the blender, on purée speed , process 25 g freshly cooked beetroot until really smooth. Add to the mixer bowl with the rest of the ingredients.

LINGUINE WITH GARLIC, OIL AND CHILLI

This classic Italian sauce is so simple it allows you to appreciate the flavour and texture of the strands of very fine home-made linguine.

SERVES 4

Preparation time: 20 minutes

Cooking time: 10 minutes

Attachments used

1 quantity basic pasta dough (page 38), rolled out to a setting 6 to 8 thickness

For the sauce

6–8 Tbsp extra-virgin olive oil

2–4 cloves garlic, finely chopped

1/2 tsp dried chilli flakes

Salt and freshly ground black pepper

Freshly shaved Parmesan cheese

2–3 Tbsp chopped fresh flat-leaf parsley

1 Attach the linguine fini cutter to the pasta maker and feed through the sheets of pasta dough on speed 2, cutting the strands to a spaghetti-length with scissors as they come through. Lay in a single layer on a clean tea towel or over a pasta drying rack if cooking immediately. If you want to use the pasta more than an hour after cutting it, toss it in a little flour to keep the linguine from sticking together and wrap the strands round to form nests. Leave on a tea towel to dry, then store in an airtight tin.

2 Heat the oil in a heavy-based pan and add the garlic and chilli flakes, cook gently for 5 minutes then add the seasoning. Remove from the heat and cover with a lid.

3 Cook the linguine in plenty of lightly salted boiling water for 1 to 2 minutes or until tender to the bite, al dente. Drain and return to the pan, then add the garlic/chilli-infused oil and heat through for 1 to 2 minutes, tossing lightly until the pasta is evenly coated with the flavoured oil. Sprinkle with the shaved Parmesan and chopped parsley. Serve with plenty of warm bread.

TAGLIATELLE WITH PARMESAN AND CORIANDER SAUCE

This speckled tagliatelle is slightly spicy and is served with a simple coriander pesto made with lots of Parmesan cheese.

SERVES 4 TO 6

Preparation time: 20 minutes plus

1 hour chilling time

Cooking time: 3 minutes

Attachments used

Blender used

450 g 00, durum wheat or plain flour

5 medium eggs

1 tsp turmeric

1 tsp paprika

1 Tbsp black pepper

For the Parmesan and coriander sauce

150 g Parmesan cheese, grated

2 Tbsp fresh coriander leaves

2 Tbsp pine kernels

Sea salt

2 Tbsp olive oil

1 Place the flour, eggs, turmeric, paprika and black pepper in the mixer bowl and attach the flat beater. On speed 1, mix slowly until the mixture is thoroughly incorporated. Exchange the flat beater for the dough hook and gradually increase the speed to 4, kneading for 5 to 8 minutes until a smooth, elastic pasta dough is formed. Wrap in clingfilm and leave to chill in the refrigerator for at least 1 hour.

2 Attach the pasta roller to the mixer and set the adjustment knob to 1. Cut the dough into eight pieces and pass one portion very slowly through the roller at speed 2, then fold it in half. Do this four to five times. When the dough is no longer sticky, set the adjustment knob to 2 and pass the pasta through, but do not fold the dough this time. Continue rolling the dough through four to five times on each setting until setting 5 is reached. Repeat with the other portions of dough.

3 Attach the fettuccine tagliatelle cutter to the pasta maker and feed through the sheets of pasta dough on speed 2, cutting the strands to a spaghetti-length with scissors as they come through. Lay in a single layer on a clean tea towel or over a pasta drying rack if cooking immediately. If you want to use the pasta more than an hour after cutting it, toss it in a little flour to keep the tagliatelle from sticking together and wrap the strands round to form nests. Leave on a tea towel to dry, then store in an airtight tin.

4 Using a mortar and pestle or the blender, process the Parmesan, coriander leaves, pine kernels, a little sea salt and the olive oil at stir speed until well combined.

5 Cook the tagliatelle in plenty of lightly salted boiling water for 3 minutes or until tender to the bite, al dente. Drain, mix with the Parmesan and coriander sauce and serve immediately.

AUBERGINE AND PARMESAN LASAGNE A classic lasagne dish, with the delicious Italian

combination of ripe tomatoes, aubergines cooked in olive oil, Parmesan and mozzarella cheeses.

 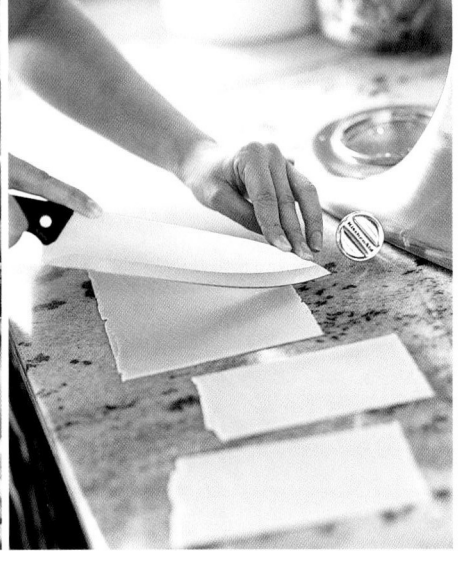

To make the pasta dough easy to handle, divide it into manageable

portions about the size of eggs, then flatten each piece out a little before

feeding it slowly through the roller. While you roll and cut out each portion

of dough, keep the rest of the portions covered with some clingfilm to

stop them drying out.

SERVES 4 TO 6

Preparation time: 30 minutes

Cooking time: 45 minutes

Attachments used

1 quantity basic pasta dough (page 38), rolled out to a setting 7 thickness
1 quantity tomato passata (page 37)
1 quantity béchamel sauce (page 36)

100 g Parmesan cheese
6–8 Tbsp extra-virgin olive oil
1.2 kg aubergines, chopped
350 g mozzarella cheese, diced

1 Preheat the oven to 220ºC/Gas Mark 7. Lay the sheets of rolled-out pasta onto a floured surface and cut into rectangular sheets, about 15 x 7 cm.

2 Bring a large saucepan of lightly salted water to the boil and cook two to three sheets of pasta for 1 minute, then plunge into cold water that has had a little olive oil added. Drain well on clean tea towels and reserve. Repeat until all the pasta sheets have been blanched. Cover with clean tea towels to prevent the pasta from drying out.

3 Attach the fine shredding drum to the rotary slicer/shredder and, on speed 4, grate the Parmesan cheese.

4 Stir the tomato sauce and one third of the béchamel sauce together, then stir in 40 g of the grated Parmesan cheese.

5 Heat 4 tablespoons of the olive oil and gently sauté the aubergines for 10 minutes or until tender, stirring frequently. Add more oil as necessary to prevent the aubergines sticking to the pan.

6 Place a layer of lasagne sheets in the base of a large greased gratin dish. Spoon over the tomato sauce mixture, sprinkle over the mozzarella and then the aubergine. Cover with the remaining lasagne sheets, spoon over the remaining béchamel sauce and sprinkle with the remaining Parmesan cheese. Bake in the oven for 20 to 25 minutes or until golden brown and bubbly, and thoroughly heated through.

PEPPERS AND BROCCOLI LASAGNE A vegetarian lasagne, this dish is hearty, with

cannellini beans making up the sauce along with fresh vegetables. Instead of a tomato sauce, it is topped with slices of fresh tomato.

SERVES 4 TO 6

Preparation time: 30 minutes

Cooking time: 40 minutes

Attachments used

1 quantity basic pasta dough (page 38), rolled out to a setting 7 thickness

1 quantity béchamel sauce (page 36)

2 carrots

1 red pepper, deseeded

1 yellow pepper, deseeded

175 g broccoli florets

100 g French beans, cut into small lengths

400-g can cannellini beans, drained and rinsed

50 g Parmesan cheese

4 firm tomatoes, sliced

3 medium eggs

135 ml/$^1/_2$ cup thick yoghurt

1 Preheat the oven to 190°C/Gas Mark 5. Lay the sheets of rolled-out pasta onto a floured surface and cut into rectangular sheets, about 15 x 7 cm.

2 Bring a large saucepan of lightly salted water to the boil and cook two to three sheets of pasta for 1 minute, then plunge into cold water that has had a little olive oil added. Drain well on clean tea towels and reserve. Repeat until all the pasta sheets have been blanched. Cover with clean tea towels to prevent the pasta from drying out.

3 Using the rotary slicer/shredder with the slicing drum attached, on speed 4, slice the carrots and peppers. Cut the broccoli into small florets, then plunge the broccoli into boiling water together with the French beans. Cook for 2 minutes, then drain and refresh in cold water. Drain again, and add to the carrots and peppers with the cannellini beans.

4 Changing to the fine shredding drum, still on speed 4, grate the Parmesan cheese.

5 Place half the béchamel sauce in the base of a lightly oiled gratin dish and top with half the vegetables. Cover with four lasagne sheets and repeat the layering, ending with the lasagne.

6 Arrange the tomato slices over the pasta. Beat the eggs and yoghurt together, pour over the tomatoes and sprinkle with the Parmesan. Bake in the oven for 25 to 30 minutes, or until golden brown and bubbly, and thoroughly heated through, then serve immediately.

CRAB AND SPRING ONION CANNELLONI
If you are fortunate enough to live in an area where freshly caught crabs are available, this recipe is a must for you. However, it is possible to use canned or frozen crab, just ensure that you squeeze out all the excess moisture.

SERVES 4 TO 6

Preparation time: 30 minutes

Cooking time: 35 minutes

Attachments used

1 quantity basic pasta dough (page 38), rolled out to a setting 6 thickness'
1 quantity tomato passata (page 37)

6 spring onions, trimmed and chopped
2–3 small jalapeño chillies, deseeded
3 firm tomatoes, peeled and deseeded
300 g white crab meat
Salt and freshly ground black pepper
50 g Gruyère cheese
Fresh parsley sprigs, to garnish

1 Preheat the oven to 190°C/Gas Mark 5. Lay the sheets of rolled-out pasta onto a floured surface and cut into rectangular sheets, about 15 x 7 cm.

2 Bring a large saucepan of lightly salted water to the boil and cook two to three sheets of pasta for 1 minute, then plunge into cold water that has had a little olive oil added. Drain well on clean tea towels and reserve. Repeat until all the pasta sheets have been blanched. Cover with clean tea towels to prevent the pasta from drying out.

3 Using the rotary slicer/shredder, fitted with the medium shredding drum, on speed 4, mince the spring onions, chillies and tomatoes into the mixer bowl. Add the crab meat, with seasoning to taste, and mix together.

4 Change to the fine shredding drum and, still on speed 4, grate the cheese.

5 Place about 2 tablespoons of the filling at one end of a lasagne sheet. Moisten the edges and roll up to encase the filling. Place the filled tubes, seam-side down, into the base of a greased ovenproof dish. Pour over the tomato sauce, sprinkle with the cheese, then bake in the oven for 25 minutes or until golden and bubbly. Garnish with the parsley sprigs.

SPINACH, MUSHROOM AND RICOTTA CANNELLONI

Sheets of home-made fresh pasta are quick to roll up into great cannelloni tubes. This spinach, mushroom and ricotta filling would work equally well in ravioli or lasagne.

SERVES 4 TO 6

Preparation time: 30 minutes

Cooking time: 35 minutes

Attachments used

1 quantity basic pasta dough (page 38), rolled out to a setting 6 thickness

1 quantity tomato passata (page 37)

1 Tbsp olive oil

1 small onion, chopped

75 g mushrooms, finely chopped

225 g ricotta cheese

225 g frozen spinach, thawed

$1/4$–$1/2$ tsp freshly grated nutmeg

Salt and freshly ground black pepper

50 g mozzarella cheese

1 Preheat the oven to 190°C/Gas Mark 5. Lay the sheets of rolled-out pasta onto a floured surface and cut into rectangular sheets, about 15 x 7 cm.

2 Bring a large saucepan of lightly salted water to the boil and cook two to three sheets of pasta for 1 minute, then plunge into cold water that has had a little olive oil added. Drain well on clean tea towels and reserve. Repeat until all the pasta sheets have been blanched. Cover with clean tea towels to prevent the pasta from drying out.

3 Heat the oil in a small pan and sauté the onion and mushrooms for 5 minutes. Drain and reserve.

4 With the flat beater on speed 4, beat the ricotta cheese in the mixer bowl until soft and creamy, then beat in the onion mixture. Squeeze out any excess moisture from the spinach and beat into the cheese, with the nutmeg and seasoning to taste.

5 Using the rotary slicer/shredder, fitted with the fine shredding drum, on speed 4, grate the mozzarella cheese.

6 Place about 2 tablespoons of the filling at one end of a lasagne sheet. Moisten the edges and roll up to encase the filling. Place the filled tubes, seam-side down, into the base of a greased ovenproof dish. Pour over the tomato sauce and sprinkle with the mozzarella, then bake in the oven for 25 minutes or until golden and bubbly.

RAVIOLI

These fat squares of Italian fresh pasta are filled with a pork, red wine and herb filling. Here they are served with a tomato sauce and Parmesan cheese, but you could just pour over melted butter and a handful of freshly chopped herbs.

SERVES 4 TO 6

Preparation time: 30 minutes plus
1 hour standing time
Cooking time: 40 minutes

Attachments used

1 quantity basic pasta dough (page 38), rolled out to a setting 6 thickness
1 quantity tomato passata (page 37)

1 onion
1 carrot
1 celery stalk
1 large clove garlic
90 g lean pork or veal, trimmed and cut into chunks
90 g prosciutto
1 Tbsp chopped fresh oregano leaves
Salt and freshly ground black pepper
1 Tbsp olive oil
3–4 Tbsp red wine or stock
50 g Parmesan cheese
Flour, for dusting

1 Using the rotary slicer/shredder, with the medium shredding drum attached, on speed 4, chop the onion, carrot, celery and garlic into the mixer bowl.

2 Change to the food grinder, with the fine grinding plate attached, on speed 4, and mince the pork or veal and the prosciutto into the bowl with the vegetables. Add the oregano and seasoning to taste and mix well.

3 Heat the oil in a large pan and gently cook the meat and vegetables with the wine or stock for 20 to 30 minutes, or until cooked, stirring frequently and taking care not to let the mixture dry out or burn. Remove, drain and leave until cool.

4 Attach the fine shredding drum to the rotary slicer/shredder and, on speed 4, grate the Parmesan.

5 Lay the sheets of rolled-out pasta onto a floured surface and cut into rectangular sheets, about 15 x 7 cm.

6 Place one strip of pasta on the lightly floured surface. Put the filling in a piping bag fitted with a large potato nozzle or use a teaspoon to place teaspoonfuls on the filling at 5-cm intervals on the pasta.

7 Moisten the edges of another piece of pasta and place it on top to encase the fillings. Sprinkle with a little flour and leave for about 1 hour. Repeat with the remaining pasta sheets and filling.

8 Using a pasta wheel or knife, cut at 5-cm intervals between the fillings to make squares. Cut along all the edges to give a fluted edge and pinch the edges firmly together.

9 Cook the ravioli in plenty of lightly salted boiling water for 3 to 4 minutes or until tender to the bite, al dente. Drain well then return to the pan, add the tomato sauce and heat through. Serve immediately with Parmesan.

SCHWÄBISCHE MAULTASCHEN (Beef and pork pockets) Little ravioli from the south of Germany,

which are usually served in a broth with a sprinkling of herbs as a starter, but can also be sprinkled with onion rings fried in a little butter until golden.

SERVES 4

Preparation time: 45 minutes plus 30 minutes standing time

Cooking time: 20 minutes

Attachments used

1 quantity basic pasta dough (page 38), rolled out to a setting 6 to 7 thickness

1 bread roll

200 g good-quality beef, such as rump or blade

50 g smoked back bacon

1 small onion

100 g pork sausagemeat

1 tsp butter

200 g fresh spinach

1 Tbsp chopped fresh parsley

1 medium egg

Salt and freshly ground black pepper

1/2 tsp freshly grated nutmeg

1.2 litres beef stock

2 Tbsp snipped fresh chives

1 Cover the bread roll with cold water and leave to one side. Trim the beef and cut into strips. Using the food grinder, fitted with the fine grinding plate, on speed 4, mince the beef, bacon and onion into the mixer bowl. Add the sausagemeat and mix well with the flat beater on speed 2.

2 Heat the butter in a frying pan and sauté the meat mixture for 5 minutes, stirring frequently until browned. Cover the spinach with boiling water, drain thoroughly and squeeze out any excess moisture. Squeeze out the moisture from the bread roll, then add the spinach, parsley and the bread roll to the meat mixture. Beat the egg, then add to the meat with seasoning to taste and the nutmeg. Mix well with the flat beater on speed 2.

3 Lay the sheets of rolled-out pasta onto a floured surface and, using a 6-cm pastry cutter, cut the dough into rounds. Place a spoonful of the prepared filling in the centre of each round, moisten the edges and fold over to form a semi-circle. Press the edges firmly together. Cover and leave to dry for 30 minutes.

4 Bring the beef stock to the boil, then drop a few of the filled pockets into the stock and cook gently for 10 to 15 minutes. Drain and keep warm while cooking the remaining pockets. When all the pockets are cooked, return to the hot stock and serve sprinkled with the chives.

TORTELLINI WITH SMOKED SALMON AND DILL Italian tortellini

are traditionally made with meat, cheese or vegetables, but these ones are filled with smoked salmon, ricotta and dill and are served with a lemony crème fraîche sauce.

SERVES 4

Preparation time: 40 minutes plus 1 hour standing
Cooking time: 10 minutes

Attachments used

1 quantity basic pasta dough (page 38), rolled out
    to a setting 6 to 7 thickness

50 g Parmesan cheese

150 g smoked salmon

300 g ricotta cheese

2 Tbsp grated lemon rind

2 Tbsp chopped fresh dill

Salt and freshly ground black pepper

1 egg, beaten

25 g butter

6 spring onions, chopped

300 ml/1¼ cups crème fraîche or double cream

Fresh dill sprigs, to garnish

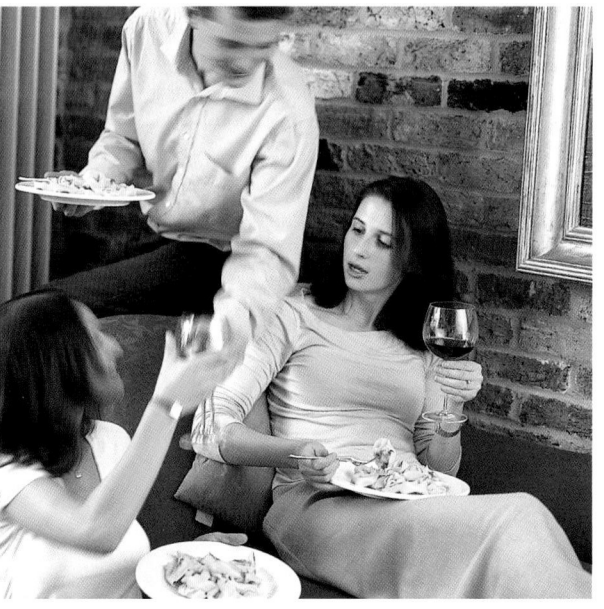

1 Using the rotary slicer/shredder, with the fine shredding drum attached, grate the Parmesan cheese on speed 4.

2 Finely chop the smoked salmon. Place the ricotta cheese into the mixer bowl and, using the flat beater, beat the ricotta cheese on speed 4 until really creamy. Add 1 tablespoon of the lemon rind, 1 tablespoon of the dill and seasoning to taste. Add the Parmesan cheese, chopped salmon and then the beaten egg, and mix gently together.

3 Lay the sheets of rolled-out pasta onto a floured surface and cut into rectangular sheets, about 15 x 7 cm. Take one strip of pasta and cut out small rounds about 6 cm in diameter. Either place the stuffing in a piping bag fitted with a large potato nozzle or place teaspoonfuls in the centre of the pasta rounds.

4 Moisten the edges of the pasta with a little water and fold over, encasing the filling. Holding a filled pasta, curve the pasta round to form a half-moon shape and pinch the pointed edges together, to form a ring. Continue until all the pasta and stuffing have been used. Sprinkle with a little flour and leave to dry for about an hour.

5 Cook the tortellini in plenty of lightly salted boiling water for 3 to 4 minutes or until tender to the bite, al dente.

6 Meanwhile, heat the butter in a small pan, add the spring onions and fry gently for 2 minutes. Add the crème fraîche or cream, the remaining lemon rind and dill, and heat gently until hot, stirring occasionally.

7 Drain the cooked tortellini, then return to the pan. Pour over the sauce and serve garnished with the dill sprigs.

SPINACH AND PARMESAN GNOCCHI This spinach and Parmesan gnocchi, known as

Roman gnocchi, is made from semolina rather than potato. It is then cooked under the grill or in the oven to make a hearty supper.

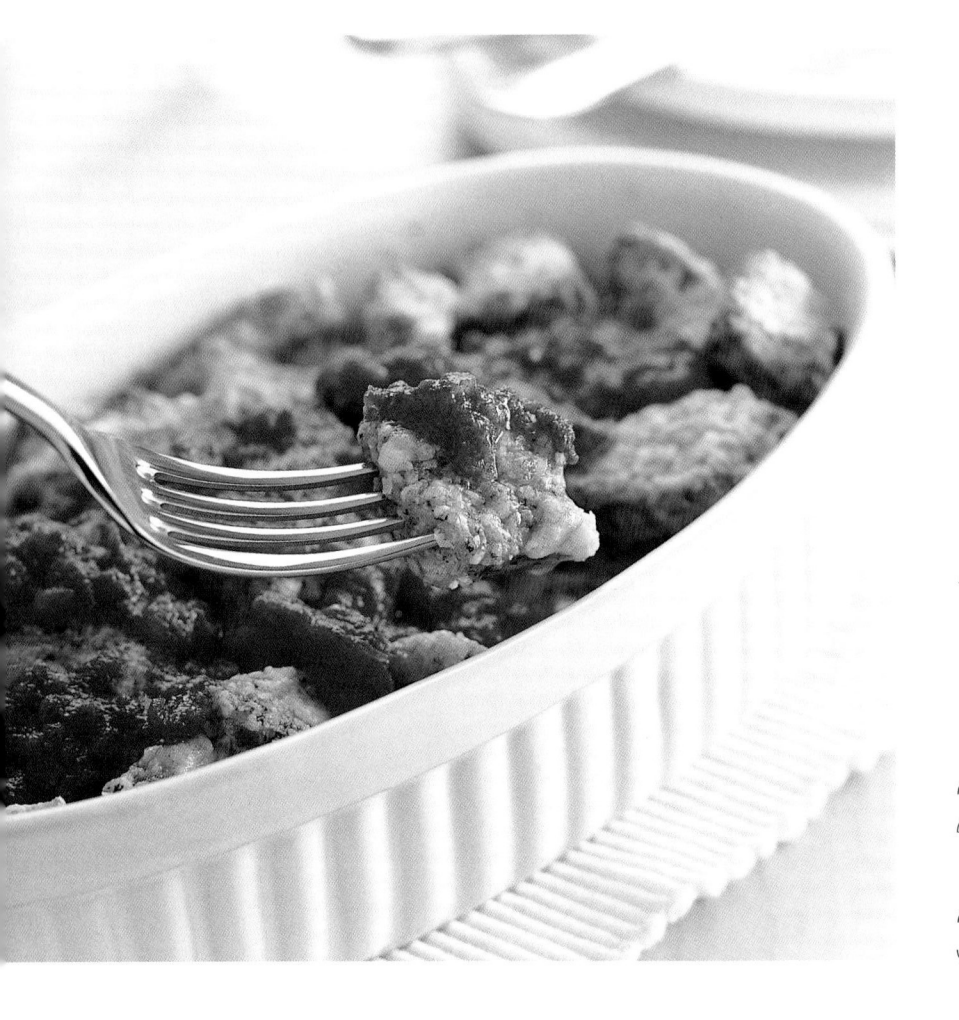

SERVES 4

Preparation time: 15 minutes

Cooking time: 20 minutes

Attachments used

50 g Parmesan cheese

300 g fresh spinach, washed thoroughly

600 ml/2^1/$_2$ cups milk

100 g semolina

50 g softened butter

2 medium eggs, beaten

Salt and freshly ground black pepper

^{1}/$_4$ tsp freshly grated nutmeg

25 g butter, melted

Tomato passata (optional)

1 With the medium shredding drum on the rotary slicer/shredder, on speed 4, grate the Parmesan. Place the spinach, with just the water clinging to the leaves, into a saucepan and cook for 3 to 4 minutes or until just wilted. Drain thoroughly and chop finely, then place in kitchen paper and squeeze out any excess moisture.

2 Pour the milk into a heavy-based pan and bring to the boil. Sprinkle in the semolina and stir until the mixture becomes really thick. Turn into the mixer bowl.

3 Add half the Parmesan, the spinach and the softened butter. Using the flat beater, on speed 6, beat well, then gradually pour in the eggs and beat well. Add some seasoning with the nutmeg, then turn into a lightly oiled shallow dish. Leave until cold.

4 Cut the cold gnocchi into small rounds about 2 cm in size. Place in an oiled shallow gratin or baking dish and pour over the melted butter. Place under a preheated medium grill and cook for 10 to 15 minutes or until heated through and golden brown. Sprinkle with the remaining Parmesan and serve with tomato passata.

FETTUCCINE ALLA ROMANA
A creamy pasta dish 'in the Roman style', which in this case means a sauce made with hot pancetta, local white wine and lots of cream and Parmesan.

SERVES 4

Preparation time: 20 minutes

Cooking time: 20 minutes

Attachments used

1 quantity basic pasta dough (page 38), rolled out to a setting 7 thickness

50 g Parmesan cheese

4 tsp extra-virgin olive oil

2 tsp butter

1 clove garlic, crushed

$1/2$ tsp paprika

150 g pancetta or streaky bacon, chopped

150 ml/$2/3$ cup white wine

120 ml/$1/2$ cup single cream

1 Attach the fettuccine tagliatelle cutter to the pasta maker and feed through the sheets of pasta dough on speed 2, cutting the strands to a spaghetti-length with scissors as they come through. Lay in a single layer on a clean tea towel or over a pasta drying rack if cooking immediately. If you want to use the pasta more than an hour after cutting it, toss it in a little flour to keep the fettuccine from sticking together and wrap the strands round to form nests. Leave on a tea towel to dry, then store in an airtight tin.

2 Using the rotary slicer/shredder, with the fine shredding drum attached, on speed 4, grate the Parmesan cheese.

3 Meanwhile, heat the olive oil and butter in a saucepan and sauté the garlic, paprika and bacon for 5 minutes or until softened. Add the wine and cream, bring to the boil, then reduce the heat and simmer for 10 minutes or until slightly reduced.

4 Cook the fettuccine in plenty of lightly salted boiling water for 1 to 2 minutes or until tender to the bite, al dente. Drain, stir into the sauce and heat thoroughly. Serve immediately with the grated Parmesan.

SPÄTZLE (German noodles) A cross between noodles and dumplings, these German spätzle are served with fried onions. If you prefer you can scatter them with golden breadcrumbs cooked in butter.

SERVES 4

Preparation time: 15 minutes plus 15 minutes standing time

Cooking time: 15 minutes

Attachments used

300 g plain flour

Pinch of freshly grated nutmeg

Salt and freshly ground black pepper

3 eggs

About 150 ml/^{2}/$_3$ cup cold water

1 large onion, cut into wedges

2 tsp oil

25 g unsalted butter

1 Sieve the flour into the mixer bowl. Add the nutmeg and season generously with salt and pepper.

2 Beat the eggs in a jug with 120 ml/^{1}/$_2$ cup of the water. With the flat beater on speed 1, gradually add the egg mixture to make a smooth thick batter, adding the remaining water if needed. Cover the bowl and leave to stand for 15 minutes.

3 Meanwhile, using the rotary slicer/shredder with the slicing drum attached, on speed 4, finely slice the onion. Melt the oil and butter in a large frying pan and gently cook the onion for 10 to 15 minutes, or until very soft and just beginning to colour.

4 Preheat the oven to its lowest setting. Bring a large pan of lightly salted water to a fast boil. Spread the dough thinly over a damp wooden chopping board.

5 Using a wet long knife, cut the dough into narrow strips and slide them off the corner of the board into the water. As soon as the noodles float to the surface, remove from the water with a slotted spoon, transfer to a heatproof dish and keep warm in the oven.

6 When all the noodles are made, scatter with the fried onions and serve straight away.

FISH, MEAT AND POULTRY DISHES

CRAB CAKES WITH MANGO SAMBAL
These spicy crab cakes are made with fresh coriander and lemon grass and are accompanied by a home-made Southeast Asian fruit sambal, or chutney.

SERVES 4

Preparation time: 15 minutes

Cooking time: 10 minutes

Attachments used

For the sambal

½ ripe mango

1 ripe avocado

1 spring onion, finely chopped

1 small bird's eye chilli or Thai chilli, seeds removed and finely chopped

1 tsp Thai fish sauce

2 Tbsp lime juice

½ tsp sugar

1 Tbsp finely chopped fresh coriander

½ Tbsp finely chopped fresh parsley

For the crab cakes

250 g white crab meat, well drained

2 spring onions, including green tops, finely chopped

2 Tbsp finely chopped fresh coriander

2 tsp lime juice

1 tsp light soy sauce

1 tsp Thai fish sauce

1 red bird's eye chilli or Thai chilli, finely chopped

1 stalk lemon grass, finely chopped

1 tsp finely chopped fresh ginger

1 large egg white

1 Tbsp cornflour

Sunflower or vegetable oil, for shallow frying

Lime quarters, to serve

1 To prepare the sambal, chop the mango and avocado into 6-mm dice, then add the remaining ingredients and mix well. Set aside until needed.

2 Using the flat beater on speed 2, mix all the crab cake ingredients together except the egg white and cornflour. Transfer to another bowl and set aside.

3 Clean the mixer bowl and dry thoroughly, then whisk the egg white and cornflour together with the wire whip on speed 8 until white and fluffy but not firm. Fold the egg whites gently into the crab mixture using a metal spoon, ensuring that it is well blended.

4 Form the mixture into four large, round patties or into 16 small ones. Heat about 1 cm of oil in a heavy-based frying pan and cook the crab cakes for about two minutes on each side, or one minute for the small cakes, until golden. Serve immediately with the mango and avocado sambal and lime quarters.

TERRINE OF FISH
All around the Mediterranean you find wonderful fish recipes like this simple Spanish fish terrine. It can be made with any white fish and is served in slices with a spoon of home-made mayonnaise.

SERVES 8

Preparation time: 10 minutes

Cooking time: 1 hour 25 minutes

Attachments used

500 g white fish fillets, skinned

1 leek, roughly chopped

1 carrot, roughly chopped

8 eggs

Pinch of salt

Pinch of white pepper

250 ml/1 cup double cream

250 ml/1 cup tomato passata (page 37)

25 g fresh white breadcrumbs

Sprigs of dill, to garnish

Mayonnaise, to serve (page 22)

1 Preheat the oven to 180°C/Gas Mark 4. Put the fish in a large frying pan and cover with water. Add the leek and carrot to the pan and cook over a medium heat for 10 minutes until the fish is cooked through. Remove the fish with a fish slice and leave to cool. Discard the vegetables and cooking liquid.

2 Flake the fish, removing any bones. Put the eggs in the mixer bowl with the fish, salt and pepper, cream and tomato sauce. With the flat beater, mix on speed 1 for 1 minute until well blended.

3 Lightly butter a 1-litre bread tin and coat the inside with the breadcrumbs. Spoon the fish mixture into the tin and cover with foil. Put the loaf tin into a roasting tin half-filled with boiling water and cook in this bain-marie for 1 hour 15 minutes, or until set and cooked through. Unmould the loaf, slice, garnish with dill, and serve with mayonnaise.

GEDDE BOLLEN (Fish balls) These tasty little Norwegian fish balls are made here with cod and are usually served with the creamy dill sauce poured over them and a serving of boiled potatoes and simple buttered vegetables.

SERVES 4

Preparation time: 20 minutes plus 1 hour 30 minutes chilling time

Cooking time: 8 minutes

Attachments used

3 slices (about 125 g) day-old white bread, crusts discarded

3 Tbsp double cream

3 Tbsp milk

350 g white fish fillet, such as cod, skinned and cut into strips

100 g butter

2 eggs

Pinch of freshly grated nutmeg

Salt and freshly ground black pepper

600 ml/2^1/$_2$ cups fish stock

For the sauce

4 Tbsp double cream

2 Tbsp chopped fresh parsley or dill

1 Break the bread into small pieces and put in a saucepan. Drizzle over the cream and milk, then leave to soak for about 5 minutes.

2 Attach the food grinder, fitted with the fine grinding plate and, on speed 4, mince the fish into the mixer bowl.

3 Add about 1 tablespoon of the butter to the bread mixture in the saucepan, then stir over a low heat until it forms a smooth mixture that leaves the sides of the pan.

4 Add the bread to the minced fish in the mixer bowl, with the eggs, nutmeg, and some salt and pepper. Mix together using the flat beater, on speed 2, until evenly blended.

5 Place the remaining butter in a saucepan and melt over a low heat. Using the flat beater, still on speed 2, slowly trickle the butter over the fish mixture in a steady stream until you have a smooth soft purée. Cover the mixer bowl and chill for at least one hour.

6 With dampened hands, shape the mixture into 20 small balls, each about the size of a walnut, and put them on a lightly floured plate. Chill them for a further 30 minutes, or freeze them briefly to make them very firm.

7 Bring the fish stock to the boil in a wide shallow saucepan or frying pan, then reduce the heat so that it is gently simmering. Add the fish balls and poach for 7 to 8 minutes, turning them over halfway through. Using a slotted spoon, lift the fish balls into a serving dish and keep warm.

8 For the sauce, rapidly boil the stock until it reduces to about 100 ml/ ^{1}/$_2$ cup. Stir in the cream and fresh herbs and simmer for 2 minutes. Taste and season with a little salt and pepper, then drizzle over the fish balls.

LAKSA

A spicy noodle soup from Southeast Asia, found all over Malaysia and Singapore, and made from chicken or seafood. Laksa is a meal in itself and is eaten with chopsticks and a spoon to scoop up all the tasty broth.

SERVES 4

Preparation time: 15 minutes

Cooking time: 25 minutes

Attachments used

1 large carrot

1 red pepper, deseeded

1 yellow pepper, deseeded

1–2 bird's eye chillies, deseeded

2 lemon grass stalks, outer leaves discarded

2 cloves garlic

2-cm piece root ginger

600 ml/2^1/$_2$ cups coconut milk

300 ml/1^1/$_4$ cups chicken stock

Few saffron strands

Two 150 g-skinless, boneless chicken breasts, cut into thin strips

175 g medium egg noodles

2 Tbsp cornflour

Handful of chopped fresh coriander leaves

175 g peeled prawns, thawed if frozen

1 Attach the coarse shredding drum to the rotary slicer/shredder and, on speed 4, slice the carrot and the red and yellow peppers.

2 Replace the coarse shredding drum with the medium shredding drum and, on speed 4, chop the chillies, lemon grass, garlic and ginger. Pour the coconut milk into a wok or saucepan with the stock and then add the chopped chilli mixture. Simmer for 10 minutes.

3 Add the saffron strands with the carrot, pepper and the chicken to the pan and bring to the boil, then simmer for a further 5 minutes.

4 Meanwhile, break the noodles into short lengths and cook in lightly boiling water for 5 minutes, drain and keep warm.

5 Blend the cornflour to a paste with 2 tablespoons of water, then stir into the wok or pan. Cook, stirring, until the mixture thickens. Stir in the chopped coriander and the prawns, cook for 2 minutes, or until the prawns are thoroughly heated, then add the noodles and serve.

PRAWN AND SPRING ONION CRÊPES

These Asian pancakes can be filled with chicken or vegetables instead of prawns. They can be prepared ahead, stored in the refrigerator and heated through before adding the filling.

SERVES 4

Preparation time: 15 minutes plus 30 minutes standing time

Cooking time: 30 minutes

Attachments used

For the batter

100 g plain flour

Pinch of salt

$1/2$–1 tsp mild chilli powder

1 medium egg, beaten

250 ml/1 cup milk

2–3 Tbsp sunflower oil, for frying

For the filling

400-g can chopped tomatoes

6 spring onions, chopped

2 celery stalks, finely chopped

1 Tbsp sweet chilli sauce, or to taste

2 Tbsp chopped fresh coriander

1 Tbsp cornflour

300 g peeled prawns, thawed if frozen

Salt and freshly ground black pepper

Fresh herbs, to garnish

1 Sieve the flour, salt and chilli powder into the mixer bowl, make a well in the centre and pour in the beaten egg. Using the flat beater, on speed 2 to 4, gradually mix in the milk, stopping to scrape down the sides of the bowl as necessary. Continue to beat until a smooth batter is formed. Leave to stand for 30 minutes.

2 To make the filling, pour the tomatoes into a pan and add the spring onion, celery, sweet chilli sauce and chopped coriander. Simmer for 3 minutes, then blend the cornflour with 2 tablespoons of water and stir into the pan. Keep stirring until thickened. Mix in the peeled prawns and add seasoning to taste. Keep warm.

3 Heat a small frying pan and pour in a little of the oil. Swirl the frying pan so that the base is completely coated with the hot oil, pouring off any

excess. Stir the batter, then pour 3 to 4 tablespoons into the pan and swirl to coat the base evenly. Cook for 2 minutes or until the bubbles on the top of the pancake burst, then turn the pancake over and cook the other side for 1 minute or until done. Remove to a plate and stack between pieces of greaseproof paper. Keep warm while you make the rest of the panckaes.

4 Fill the cooked pancakes with the prawn and spring onion sauce and serve garnished with fresh herbs.

POACHED SALMON
This spectacular British summer dish is a grand addition to any table and is ideal for a buffet party or to serve at a formal lunch. Accompany with home-made mayonnaise.

The rotary slicer/shredder copes well with big quantities, but even if you are chopping, slicing, or grating more than just one or two vegetables, using this attachment rather than doing it by hand will save you time and effort. Here the slicing drum also produces beautifully even, wafer-thin slices of cucumber for decoration.

SERVES 10 TO 12

Preparation time: 30 minutes

Cooking time: 40 minutes

Attachments used

1.75 kg whole salmon, gutted

1 onion, sliced

1 lemon, sliced

2 celery stalks, sliced

Few fresh parsley stalks

2 bay leaves

150 ml/^{2}/$_3$ cup medium-dry white wine

900 ml/3^3/$_4$ cups water

1 very large or 2 small cucumbers, peeled or unpeeled

Salad leaves and lemon wedges, to garnish

Home-made mayonnaise, to serve (page 22)

1 Lightly rinse the salmon and pat dry with kitchen paper. Leave the skin on the fish as this helps to keep the fish intact during cooking.

2 With the slicing drum on the rotary slicer/shredder, on speed 4, slice the onion, lemon, and celery. Place, along with the parsley and bay leaves, in a fish kettle or large saucepan. Add the wine with the water and bring to the boil. Reduce the heat and simmer for 10 minutes.

3 Place the fish on the fish kettle trivet or in a tinfoil sling, lower into the simmering liquid and bring to the boil. Calculate the cooking time by allowing 10 minutes per 450 g, then simmer the fish for this amount of time. Remove from the heat and leave until cold in the cooking liquor.

4 When cold, remove the salmon from the fish kettle and carefully peel off the skin using the back of a knife, discarding also the gills and eyes. Snip the backbone at the head and tail, then carefully ease the bone out. Place the fish on a serving platter.

5 With the slicing drum on the rotary slicer/shredder, on speed 4, slice the cucumber and arrange over the salmon, to represent scales. Garnish around the base with salad leaves and lemon wedges, and serve with home-made mayonnaise.

CHICKEN, PEPPER AND MUSHROOM PARCELS These little parcels are

ideal for an informal lunch or supper party. Provided the chicken is fresh, the parcels can be made ahead of time and frozen.

SERVES 4

Preparation time: 25 minutes plus 30 minutes chilling time

Cooking time: 30 minutes

Attachments used

For the pastry

225 g plain flour

Pinch of salt

150 g unsalted butter or margarine

1 small egg yolk

2 tsp cold water

Beaten egg, to glaze

For the filling

3 shallots

1 clove garlic

2–3 slices (about 100 g) day-old bread, crusts discarded

40 g button mushrooms

1 small red pepper, deseeded

1 Tbsp olive oil

Salt and freshly ground black pepper

Small handful fresh chervil or tarragon, finely chopped

Four 150-g skinless, boneless chicken breasts

1 Lightly oil a baking sheet. To make the pastry, sieve the flour and salt into the mixer bowl. Cut the butter or margarine into cubes and add to the flour together with the egg yolk and cold water. Using the flat beater, on speed 2, beat for about 1 minute or until the mixture comes together and forms a ball in the centre of the bowl. Remove, knead lightly on a lightly floured surface, then wrap and chill in the refrigerator for 30 minutes.

2 Preheat the oven to 200°C/Gas Mark 6. Attach the medium shredding drum to the rotary slicer/shredder and, on speed 4, chop the shallots, garlic, bread and mushrooms. Replace the medium shredding drum with the slicing drum and slice the red pepper. Heat the oil in a pan and sauté the shallot mixture for 2 minutes. Remove from the heat, add seasoning to taste and the chopped herbs.

3 Roll the pastry out on a lightly floured surface and cut into four 20.5-cm squares. Divide the shallot mixture among the four pastry squares and place in the centre of each pastry square. Rinse the chicken and pat dry, then place on top and brush the edges of the pastry with a little beaten egg.

4 Fold the pastry over, completely encasing the chicken, and place seam-side down on the prepared baking sheet. Use any trimmings to decorate the tops of the parcels. Brush with the beaten egg, then bake in the oven for 25 to 30 minutes.

TURKEY WITH CHICKPEA PATTIES This is a version of a Moroccan tagine, using turkey rather

than chicken or lamb. A tagine is traditionally cooked in a conical-shaped dish called a tagine, but here it can be made in a saucepan.

SERVES 4

Preparation time: 15 minutes

Cooking time: 35 minutes

Attachments used

450 g skinless, boneless turkey breast, diced

1 tsp turmeric

1 tsp paprika

2 Tbsp olive oil

1 onion, cut into wedges

2–3 cloves garlic, chopped

600 ml/2^{1}/$_{2}$ cups chicken stock

75 g ready-to-eat dried apricots

1 cinnamon stick, broken in half

Salt and freshly ground black pepper

2 Tbsp cornflour

2 Tbsp toasted flaked almonds

1 Tbsp roughly chopped unsalted shelled pistachio nuts

1 Tbsp chopped fresh coriander

For the chickpea patties

400-g can chickpeas, drained and rinsed

6 spring onions

2 slices (about 75 g) day-old bread, crusts discarded

1 small red chilli, deseeded and chopped

Handful of fresh coriander leaves, chopped

Salt and freshly ground black pepper

1 small egg yolk

About 2 Tbsp plain flour

2 Tbsp olive oil

1 Coat the turkey in the turmeric and paprika. Heat the oil in a large pan and sauté the onion and garlic for 5 minutes. Add the turkey and continue to cook until the turkey is just browned.

2 Stir in the stock and bring to the boil, add the apricots, cinnamon and seasoning, cover and cook gently for 25 minutes, stirring occasionally during cooking. Blend the cornflour with 2 tablespoons water to a smooth paste, stir into the turkey and cook until slightly thickened.

3 Meanwhile, place the chickpeas in the mixer bowl and, using the flat beater, on speed 2, beat the chickpeas for a few minutes until broken down. Attach the medium shredding drum to the rotary slicer/shredder and, on speed 4 chop the spring onions with the bread. Add to the chickpeas together with the chilli, coriander and seasoning, to taste.

4 Stir the egg yolk into the mixture and mix until it comes together. Scrape out of the bowl and shape into small rounds. Coat in the flour.

5 Heat the oil in a frying pan and fry the patties on both sides for about 4 minutes, or until golden and heated through.

6 Sprinkle the turkey with the almonds, pistachio nuts and chopped coriander and serve with the chickpea patties, couscous or rice.

CHICKEN TANDOORI
This Indian dish is traditionally baked in a very hot clay tandoor oven, heated with charcoal. Barbecuing your chicken tandoori will create a similar smoky flavour and the marinade can be used to coat any meat or seafood.

SERVES 4

Preparation time: 40 minutes plus marinating time

Cooking time: 25 minutes

Attachments used

1¹/₂ Tbsp coriander seeds

1¹/₂ Tbsp cumin seeds

1 hot red chilli, such as bird's eye, deseeded

2 large cloves garlic

5-cm piece root ginger

2 Tbsp lemon juice

1 tsp garam masala

150 ml/²/₃ cup low-fat natural yoghurt

Few drops of red food colouring

Salt and freshly ground black pepper

Four 150-g skinless, boneless chicken breasts

Lime wedges and fresh herbs, to garnish

1 Dry-fry the coriander and cumin seeds for 3 to 4 minutes, stirring frequently and taking care not to burn the spices. Remove, cool, then grind in a pestle and mortar.

2 Attach the medium shredding drum to the rotary slicer/shredder and, on speed 4, grind the chilli, garlic and ginger into the mixer bowl. Stir in the ground spices, then the lemon juice and mix to a paste. Add the garam masala, the yoghurt and a few drops of food colouring to give a good red colour, then season.

3 Rinse the chicken and pat dry. Make three slashes across each breast and place in a shallow dish. Pour over the tandoori paste, cover and leave to marinate for at least 6 hours, spooning the marinade over the chicken occasionally, or, if time permits, leave overnight.

4 When ready to cook, preheat the grill and line the grill rack with tinfoil, or light the barbecue 20 minutes before cooking. Drain the chicken and cook for 20 to 25 minutes or until the chicken is cooked and the juices run clear. Turn the chicken frequently during cooking and brush occasionally with the marinade. Serve garnished with lime wedges and fresh herbs.

CHICKEN WITH PEPPERS

This tasty Southeast Asian stir-fry uses fresh kaffir lime leaves. If you have difficulty finding fresh ones, most supermarkets sell dried ones, or you could just leave them out.

SERVES 4

Preparation time: 10 minutes

Cooking time: 12 minutes

Attachments used

225 g cellophane noodles

5-cm piece root ginger

2 lemon grass stalks, outer leaves discarded

2–4 cloves garlic

1 red pepper, deseeded

1 yellow pepper, deseeded

1 green pepper. deseeded

2 carrots

Two 150-g skinless, boneless chicken breasts

2 Tbsp groundnut oil

1–2 bird's eye chillies, deseeded and chopped

2 kaffir lime leaves

2 Tbsp light soy sauce

1 Tbsp Thai fish sauce

2 Tbsp chopped fresh coriander

1 Soak the cellophane noodles in boiling water for 4 minutes, then drain and set aside until required.

2 With the medium shredding drum on the rotary slicer/shredder, on speed 4, grate the ginger, lemon grass and garlic. Change to the slicing drum and, still on speed 4, slice the peppers and then the carrots.

3 Cut the chicken into strips. Heat a wok until hot then add the oil, heat for 30 seconds and stir-fry the chilli, lime leaves, ginger, lemon grass and garlic for 1 minute. Add the chicken strips and continue to stir-fry for 3 minutes, or until browned.

4 Add the pepper and carrot and stir-fry for 4 minutes. Add the noodles and stir-fry for 2 minutes. Pour in the soy sauce and Thai fish sauce and stir-fry for another 2 minutes, or until the chicken is completely cooked through. Sprinkle with the chopped coriander and serve immediately.

LAMB EN CROÛTE
This lamb version of bœuf en croûte uses flaky pastry, but you could also use shortcrust pastry or a brioche dough to enclose the lamb and herb filling.

SERVES 8

Preparation time: 30 minutes

Cooking time: 20 minutes

Attachments used

130 g butter

Eight 110-g lamb fillets, approx. 10 cm long

Salt and freshly ground black pepper

2 Tbsp chopped fresh chervil

3 Tbsp chopped fresh tarragon

6 fresh basil leaves, chopped

1 Tbsp extra-virgin olive oil

1 quantity flaky pastry, rolled out to 8 sheets 15 x 15 cm each (page 118)

1 egg yolk

200 ml/1 cup lamb or beef stock

2 Tbsp cognac

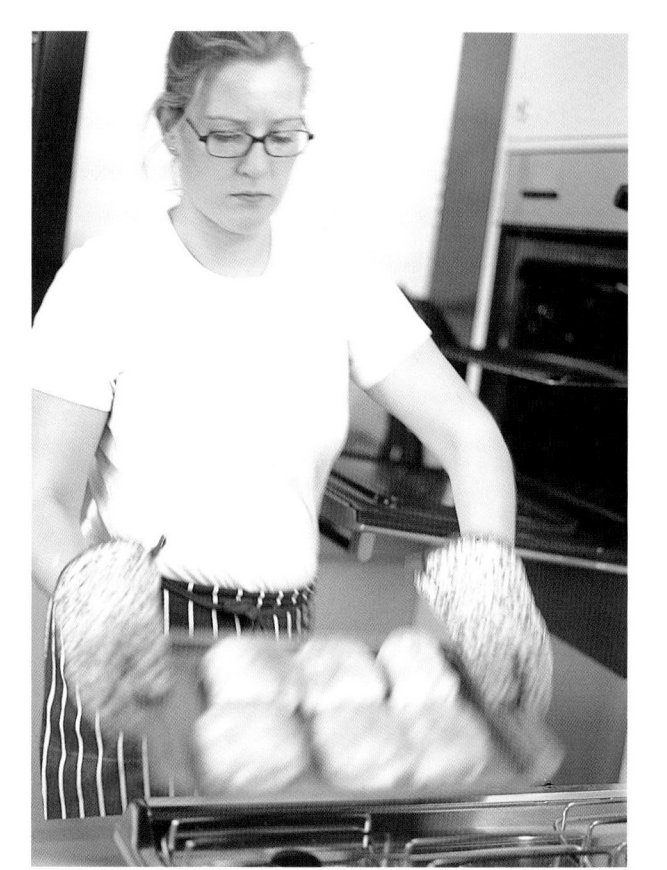

1 Preheat the oven to 200°C/Gas Mark 6. Melt 50 g of the butter in a large frying pan and rub the lamb with the salt and pepper. Sear both sides of the meat for 30 seconds on high heat. Remove from the pan immediately and drain on a wire rack or inverted plate so that the meat is not lying in its own juices. Reserve the lamb juices. Let cool and set aside.

2 In a bowl, mix together the herbs and olive oil and season with salt and pepper. The herb mixture should be a thick paste and should not be runny at all.

3 Lay out the sheets of flaky pastry. Spread 1 teaspoon of the herb mixture onto each.

4 Pat dry the lamb with kitchen paper and place one piece of meat onto each sheet of pastry. Top the meat with 1 more teaspoon of the herb mixture and fold the pastry into little parcels. Brush the ends with some cold water and seal the parcels. Turn them over and make small slits on top with a sharp knife.

5 Whisk the egg yolk with some water and brush over the lamb parcels. Place in the oven for 12 to 14 minutes until golden brown. Add the remaining butter and the cognac to the lamb juices in a small saucepan and season with salt and pepper. Heat until slightly reduced to a gravy consistency.

6 Serve the lamb parcels with the gravy and accompany with spring vegetables and parsley-buttered potatoes.

PORK WITH CALVADOS AND APPLES This version of the classic Normandy and Brittany

dish, Poulet Vallée d'Auge, is made from apples, crème fraîche and Calvados, all specialities of Northwest France.

SERVES 4

Preparation time: 15 minutes

Cooking time: 1 hour 15 minutes

Attachments used

1 onion

2–3 cloves garlic

2 cooking apples, peeled and cored

40 g unsalted butter

450 g pork fillet, cut into 1-cm slices

2 Tbsp plain flour

3 Tbsp Calvados

450 ml/1³/₄ cups chicken stock

Salt and freshly ground black pepper

1 tsp soft brown sugar

2 Tbsp chopped fresh sage

4 Tbsp crème fraîche

Apple slices, to garnish

1 Preheat the oven to 180°C/Gas Mark 4. Attach the slicing drum to the rotary slicer/shredder and, on speed 4, slice the onion and garlic, then the apples separately. Melt 25 g of the butter in a frying pan and sauté the onion and garlic for 3 minutes, add the apples and continue to sauté for a further 2 minutes. Remove with a draining spoon and reserve.

2 Heat the remaining butter in the pan, add the pork and sauté for 5 minutes, then sprinkle in the flour and cook for 2 minutes. Add the Calvados, heat for 1 minute, then draw the pan off the heat and set alight with your gas flame or a match, taking care that you stand well back and keeping a pan lid handy for emergencies. When the flames have subsided, stir in the stock, add the onion mixture and return to the heat. Cook, stirring, until the mixture thickens. Add some salt and pepper, the sugar and 1 tablespoon of the sage, and pour into a casserole.

3 Cook in the oven for 1 hour or until the pork is tender. Stir in the crème fraîche, sprinkle with the remaining sage and garnish with apple slices.

VITELLO TONNATO (Veal in tuna sauce) A northern Italian dish that needs to be made the day before and chilled overnight

in the refrigerator. If you're using a leg of veal, ask your butcher to bone it, and tie it in a neat roll.

SERVES 6

Preparation time: 25 minutes plus 24 hours
marinating and 3 hours chilling

Cooking time: 1 hour

Attachments used

1 onion, cut into wedges

1 carrot

1 stalk celery

600-g piece of leg or loin of veal

1 bay leaf

2 whole cloves

1 litre/4^1/$_2$ cups dry white wine, preferably Italian

1 tsp salt

One 200-g can tuna, drained

4 anchovy fillets, rinsed

2 Tbsp capers in vinegar

1 lemon

2 egg yolks

1 Tbsp white wine vinegar

Freshly ground black pepper

150 ml/^{2}/$_3$ cup olive oil

1 Using the rotary slicer/shredder, fitted with the slicing drum, on speed 4, slice the onion, carrot and celery into a large glass or stainless steel bowl. Make a hollow in the vegetables and put the meat in it. Add the bay leaf and cloves and pour over the wine. Cover and leave in the refrigerator for 24 hours, turning the meat several times.

2 Next day, put the meat into a saucepan with the vegetables, marinade, and the bones if you have them. Sprinkle over the salt and add just enough water to barely cover. Bring to the boil, reduce the heat, cover and simmer for 45 minutes to 1 hour, or until the meat is cooked through and tender. Remove from the heat and allow to cool in the pan.

3 Using the food grinder, with the fine grinding plate attached, on speed 4, mince the tuna, anchovy fillets and 1 tablespoon of the capers into the mixer bowl. Squeeze in the juice of half the lemon, then add the egg

yolks, vinegar and black pepper. Change to the wire whip and beat the mixture on speed 4 for a few seconds.

4 On speed 6, add the oil a little at a time in a thin stream, whisking well between each addition, until the sauce is thick and shiny. Whisk in about 2 tablespoons of the veal stock from the pan to give the sauce the consistency of thin cream. Taste and adjust the seasoning if necessary.

5 Slice the veal as thinly as possible and arrange on a serving dish. Spoon over the tuna sauce, cover and refrigerate for at least 3 hours. Serve garnished with the remaining capers and remaining lemon half, thinly sliced.

KJOTTKAKER

(Meat cakes) One of Norway's most popular dishes, these minced beef patties are made in every home to a family recipe, fried until crispy and often served with a sauce.

SERVES 4

Preparation time: 20 minutes

Cooking time: 40 minutes

Attachments used

100 g white bread, crusts discarded

2 Tbsp milk

450 g lean beef (sirloin, rump or chuck steak)

1 onion, cut into wedges

1 egg

Salt and freshly ground black pepper

2 Tbsp plain flour

2 Tbsp sunflower oil

1. Preheat the oven to 100°C/Gas Mark 1/4. Put the bread on a baking sheet and bake for 20 minutes, turning occasionally until dry.

2. Using the rotary slicer/shredder with the medium shredding drum attached, on speed 4, grate the bread into the bowl. Sprinkle over the milk and leave to soak for 5 minutes.

3. Using the food grinder, fitted with the coarse grinding plate, on speed 4, mince the beef into the bowl, followed by the onion. Add the egg and season well with salt and pepper. Mix together using the flat beater, on speed 4, until evenly blended.

4. Divide the mixture into four equal portions and shape each into an oval about 10 cm long and 5 cm wide. Lightly dust them with flour and chill if time allows.

5. Heat the oil in a frying pan and fry the meat cakes for 7 to 8 minutes on each side, or until well-browned and cooked through. Drain on kitchen paper and serve hot.

Raw meat and fish is easier to feed through the food grinder if it is cut into strips, rather than chunks. If you want your meat extra tender, you can put it through the food grinder twice, first through the coarse plate, then through the fine, although do not mince the meat twice if it is quite fatty.

FILET AMÈRICAIN WITH ORIGINAL BELGIAN FRITES The Filet

Amèricain is the perfect companion to the very finest frites in the world. In Belgium it is often served on a slice of toast, and is known as "toast cannibal".

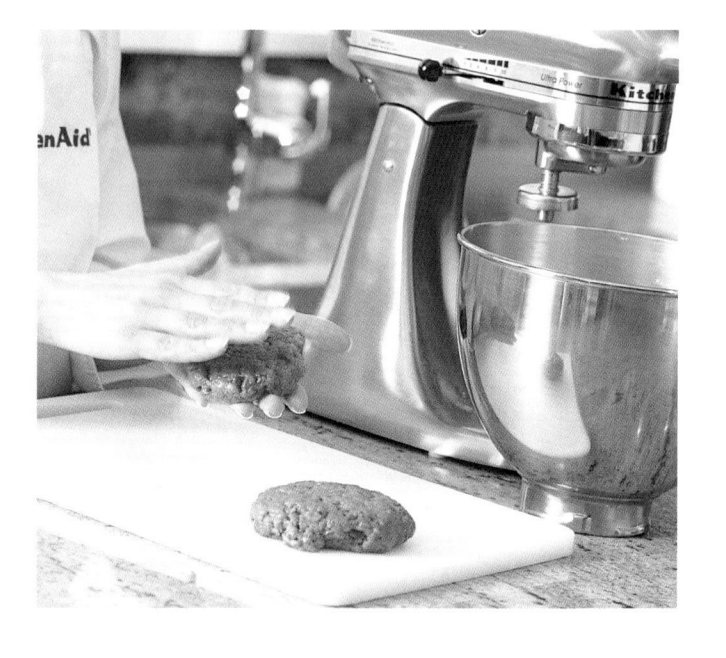

SERVES 6

Preparation time: 15 minutes, plus chilling time

Cooking time: 1 hour

Attachments used

800 g lean beef steak such as fillet or rump

12 gherkins, drained thoroughly

$1/2$ small onion, peeled

4 fresh, organic, medium egg yolks

2 Tbsp olive oil

2 Tbsp capers, drained thoroughly

1 Tbsp freshly chopped parsley

1 Tbsp Worcestershire sauce

Salt and freshly ground black pepper

For the frites

1 kg floury potatoes, peeled

Oil for deep frying

1 Trim the steak, discarding any fat or gristle and cut into strips or small cubes. Attach the food grinder fitted with the fine grinding plate and place the mixer bowl underneath. Mince the beef on speed 4 into the bowl. Do this twice so that the meat is finely ground.

2 Clean the fine plate and the food grinder and then pass the gherkins and onion through and into the mixer bowl. Add all the remaining ingredients with seasoning to taste and mix well using the flat beater.

3 Divide into 4 and shape into steaks. Cover lightly and keep in the refrigerator until required.

4 Cut the potatoes into 1 cm slices and then into thin strips. Cover completely with cold water and leave for 30 minutes to remove any excess starch. Drain thoroughly and pat dry with a clean cloth.

5 Heat the oil in a deep fryer to 190°C. Place a layer of potatoes in the frying basket and lower carefully into the hot oil. Cook for 5 minutes or until the potato frites are soft but still white. Remove and drain thoroughly. Repeat with the remaining frites.

6 Just before serving, reheat the oil to 190°C, then place a layer of the blanched frites in the frying basket. Plunge into hot oil and cook for 3 to 5 minutes or until golden brown and crisp. Remove and drain on kitchen paper and serve with the Filet Amèricain.

QUICHE LORRAINE
A speciality of the Alsace-Lorraine region of France, this quiche is made from a crisp, shortcrust pastry filled with an egg, cream, cheese and bacon mixture.

SERVES 4

Preparation time: 25 minutes plus 30 minutes chilling time

Cooking time: 50 minutes

Attachments used

200 g plain flour

Pinch of salt

100 g butter

Cold water

1 small onion, very finely chopped

4 rashers good-quality bacon, finely chopped

3 eggs, beaten

425 ml/1³/₄ cups milk, or milk and single cream mixed

75 g Gruyère cheese, finely grated

Salt and freshly ground black pepper to taste

1 Place a baking tray in the oven and preheat the oven to 220°C/ Gas Mark 7.

2 To make the pastry, sieve the flour and salt into the mixer bowl. Cut the butter into cubes. Using the flat beater, on speed 2, beat until well blended. Add just enough iced water to make a smooth dough, then remove and knead lightly on a lightly floured surface. Shape the dough into a ball, wrap in clingfilm and chill in the refrigerator for 30 minutes.

3 Roll the pastry out into a circle on a lightly floured surface and use to line a 20-cm greased tart tin, about 4 cm deep.

4 Cook the onion and bacon together for five minutes over a gentle heat in a nonstick frying pan. Spoon into the tart tin.

5 Using the flat beater on speed 4, beat the eggs into the milk, or milk and cream, then add most of the cheese with some salt and pepper and beat again. Pour the mixture over the bacon and onion and scatter the remaining cheese on top.

6 Place the quiche on the hot baking tray and bake for 10 minutes. Lower the temperature to 190°C/Gas Mark 5 and continue baking for another 30 to 35 minutes, until the filling is just set. Allow to cool slightly before cutting. Serve the quiche warm or cold.

POLPETTE

(Meatballs) These little beef meatballs are served in Italy traditionally with grilled aubergines or just some bread, as a main course, following a pasta starter. You could use pork instead of beef and basil instead of parsley.

SERVES 4

Preparation time: 20 minutes

Cooking time: 30 minutes

Attachments used

1-2 slices (about 50 g) day-old white bread, crusts discarded

50 g Parmesan cheese

1 carrot

350 g lean beef (rump or chuck steak)

1 onion, quartered

1 clove garlic

1 stalk celery

Handful fresh parsley leaves, finely chopped

1 egg

1 Tbsp olive oil

1 Preheat the oven to 140°C/Gas Mark 1. Bake the slices of bread on a baking sheet for about 20 minutes, turning several times, until dried out. Leave to cool.

2 Turn up the oven to 180°C/Gas Mark 4. Using the rotary slicer/shredder, with the fine shredding drum attached, on speed 4, grate the Parmesan into the mixer bowl. Remove 2 tablespoons of the grated cheese and set aside. Grate the bread, then the carrot, into the bowl.

3 Attach the food grinder, fitted with the fine grinding plate and, on speed 4, mince the beef into the mixer bowl, followed by the onion, garlic and celery.

4 Change to the flat beater, add the parsley, egg and olive oil to the bowl and, on speed 4, mix together until evenly blended. With dampened hands, shape the mixture into 20 small balls and place on a lightly oiled baking tray. Bake for about 30 minutes, or until piping hot and cooked through.

5 Sprinkle with the reserved Parmesan and serve immediately with grilled vegetables and perhaps some bread.

SWEDISH MEATBALLS
These spicy meatballs are made from beef and mashed potato and come with a little gravy made from the meat juices and cream. Serve them with noodles or potatoes.

SERVES 4

Preparation time: 20 minutes plus 1 hour chilling time

Cooking time: 15 minutes

Attachments used

1 onion, cut into wedges

1 medium (175 g) potato, cut into wedges

450 g lean beef (topside or blade), trimmed and cut into strips

2 Tbsp butter

3 Tbsp fine dried breadcrumbs

$1/4$ tsp dried crushed chillies

250 ml/$1^{1}/4$ cups double cream

Salt and freshly ground black pepper

1 medium egg

1 Tbsp chopped fresh parsley

3 Tbsp oil

1 Tbsp flour

1 Using the rotary slicer/shredder with the medium shredding drum attached, on speed 4, grate the onion into the mixer bowl. Remove the bowl, place a saucepan underneath the mixer and, still on speed 4, grate the potato into the pan. Cover with cold water and cook for 12 minutes or until tender. Drain the potato thoroughly, mash and reserve.

2 Attach the food grinder, fitted with the fine grinding plate and, on speed 4, mince the beef into the bowl. Do this twice so that the meat is minced finely.

3 Heat 1 tablespoon of the butter in a small saucepan and sauté the onion for 5 minutes, stirring frequently until softened, then pour into the mixer bowl. Add the breadcrumbs with the chillies, about 3 tablespoons of the double cream, the mashed potato, seasoning, egg and parsley. With the flat beater, beat the mixture on speed 6 until smooth and fluffy.

4 Shape into about 32 small meatballs and place on one or two trays. Cover with cling film and chill in the refrigerator for 1 hour.

In this recipe, the rotary slicer/shredder has prepared the onion and potato, and the grinder has minced the meat, it is then that the flat beater is used for blending the ingredients together. Unlike a food processor blade, it doesn't just keep chopping everything down.

5 When ready to cook, heat the remaining butter and oil in a frying pan. Cook the meatballs in the pan for 8 to 10 minutes or until thoroughly cooked, remove from the pan and drain well on kitchen paper.

6 Pour off the excess butter and oil from the pan, sprinkle in the flour and cook, scraping up the sediment that is left in the bottom. Pour in the remaining cream and cook, stirring, until the sauce comes to the boil. Return the meatballs to the pan and heat through gently until piping hot.

SPICY SAUSAGES

These pork sausages are used in lots of hearty winter stews, mixed with beans, lentils and tomatoes. You could roll the sausages by hand, but the sausage stuffer makes light work of producing the links.

SERVES 6

Preparation time: 30 minutes

Cooking time: 10 minutes

Attachments used

1 kg pork belly, rind and bones removed, cut into 2.5 cm cubes

2 Tbsp paprika

2 tsp dried hot pepper flakes

2 Tbsp fennel seeds

Salt and freshly ground black pepper

Natural or synthetic casings (optional)

Plain flour, for dusting (optional)

Oil, for frying

Tomato passata (page 37), to serve

1 Chill the meat before mincing in the food grinder, on speed 4, first through the coarse plate and then through the fine plate.

2 In the mixer bowl, and using the flat beater on speed 2 to 4, mix the spices and seasoning into the minced pork.

3 If using the sausage stuffer, soak the natural casings in cold water for 30 minutes, then rinse thoroughly. Grease the large sausage stuffer tube and slide the casing on tightly, tying off the end. On speed 4, feed through the pork mixture, twisting and shaping the sausages into small links. Roll the sausages in a little plain flour before cooking.

4 Heat a little oil in a frying pan and fry the sausages, turning two or three times, until browned. Serve hot, with tomato passata.

BRATWURST

A very popular pale German sausage made from a mixture of minced pork and veal. The sausages are fried or grilled and are often served with crispy fried potatoes and sauerkraut.

SERVES 3 TO 4

Preparation time: 15 minutes

Cooking time: 20 minutes

Attachments used

300 g lean pork fillet, trimmed

150 g veal escalope or lean beef (such as rump steak)

3 small shallots, peeled and cut into wedges

25 g fresh white breadcrumbs

1 tsp ground ginger

1 tsp ground coriander

$1/2$ tsp caraway seeds

$1/4$–$1/2$ tsp freshly grated nutmeg

Salt and freshly ground black pepper

6–8 natural or synthetic casings

Oil, for frying

1 Chill the meat and cut into strips before mincing in the food grinder with the shallots, on speed 4, first through the coarse plate and then through the fine plate.

2 In the mixer bowl, and using the flat beater on speed 2 to 4, mix the breadcrumbs, spices and seasoning into the minced meat.

3 Before using the sausage stuffer, soak the natural casings in cold water for 30 minutes, then rinse thoroughly. Grease the large sausage stuffer tube and slide the casing on tightly, tying off the end. On speed 4, feed through the meat mixture, twisting the sausages into small links

4 Heat a little oil in a frying pan and fry the sausages for 15 to 20 minutes, turning two or three times, until browned.

BABY CHICKEN WITH CARROTS
This recipe for baby food is a perfect introduction to grown-up tastes. It is suitable for babies over 6 months old and if you are making extra, freeze what you do not need immediately in ice cube trays, remembering to label and date it clearly.

MAKES ENOUGH FOR 4 BABY MEALS

Preparation time: 10 minutes

Cooking time: 25 minutes

Blender used

1 Tbsp butter

$1/2$ skinless, boneless chicken breast, diced

1 carrot, chopped

1 medium potato, chopped

A few broccoli florets

2 tomatoes, skinned and deseeded

300 ml/$1^1/4$ cups chicken stock

1 Heat the butter in a frying pan and sauté the chicken for 5 minutes or until browned. Add the vegetables with the tomatoes and stock and bring to the boil. Reduce the heat, cover and cook over a gentle heat for 12 minutes or until the chicken and vegetables are completely cooked through.

2 Remove from the heat, cool slightly, then mix in the blender on purée speed until the mixture reaches the right consistency. Serve immediately, and freeze any extra in ice cube trays.

BABY PEACH FOOL
This baby pudding is suitable for babies over 6 months of age. You can use almost any fresh or cooked fruit for the recipe, but try to choose fruit that is very ripe and naturally sweet.

MAKES ENOUGH FOR 2 BABY MEALS

Preparation time: 5 minutes

Blender used

1 ripe peach

3 Tbsp natural fromage frais

1 Tbsp baby rice

1 Tbsp sugar (optional)

Rusk or sponge finger biscuit (optional)

1 Plunge the peach into hot water and leave it for a few minutes. Pour away the water, carefully peel the peach and cut it in half. Discard the stone.

2 Place the peach in the blender with the fromage frais and the baby rice, and blend on purée speed until smooth.

3 Taste and, if necessary, add a little sugar. Serve with a rusk or sponge finger biscuit.

VEGETABLE DISHES

MASHED POTATOES
You can serve this mash topped with crème fraîche and scattered with chopped spring onions or chives, or lay slices of smoked salmon or baked or pan-fried cod on top for a quick meal.

SERVES 6 TO 8

Preparation time: 15 minutes

Cooking time: 20 minutes

Attachments used

1 kg potatoes (e.g. Maris Piper), cut into quarters
100 g butter, cut into small cubes
120–140 ml/$^1/_2$–$^2/_3$ cup double cream or full-fat milk
Salt and freshly ground black pepper

1 Boil the potatoes in salted water until tender, then drain them well. Place the cooked potatoes in the mixer bowl and, using the flat beater on speed 2 to 4, mash them well, then add the butter.

2 Heat the cream or milk, not allowing it to boil, and add it to the potatoes. Beat again until fluffy. Season as required with salt and black pepper and serve immediately.

COLCANNON
An Irish potato dish traditionally eaten at Halloween, colcannon is often served in individual pots with a pool of melted butter in the middle of the potato for dipping each forkful of mash into.

SERVES 8

Preparation time: 10 minutes

Cooking time: 20 minutes

Attachments used

1.4 kg potatoes
175 g butter
2 Tbsp milk
6 spring onions or 3 Tbsp chives, chopped
500 g cooked kale or green cabbage, finely chopped
Salt and freshly ground black pepper
Grated nutmeg

1 Cut the potatoes into quarters and cook in boiling water for 20 minutes until softened and cooked through. Drain well and transfer to the mixer bowl. Add the butter and milk.

2 Using the flat beater, beat together for 30 seconds on speed 2. Reduce to speed 1 and add the spring onions or chives and the kale or cabbage. Season well.

3 Spoon the colcannon into a warm serving dish, grate a little nutmeg over the top and serve.

GREEN SAUCE WITH NEW POTATOES
There is no single recipe for this well-loved German sauce, but all use the same spring herbs. Serve over new potatoes or with boiled beef, salted brisket or steamed fish.

SERVES 6

Preparation time: 15 minutes plus 30 minutes infusing and 30 minutes chilling time

Cooking time: 20 minutes

Attachments used

25 g each of fresh sorrel, salad burnet, chervil, borage, parsley and
    watercress
2 medium shallots
3 Tbsp white wine vinegar
4 medium eggs, hard boiled and shelled
300ml/1¼ cups double or single cream
Salt and freshly ground black pepper
1 Tbsp mustard
4 Tbsp olive oil
750 g new potatoes

1 Finely chop all the herbs and watercress. Using the rotary slicer/shredder fitted with the medium shredding drum, on speed 4, finely chop the shallots. Add to the herbs and pour over the vinegar, then cover and leave to stand for 30 minutes.

2 Pass the eggs through the rotary slicer/shredder fitted with the medium shredding drum, on speed 4, into the mixer bowl. Attach the flat beater and, on speed 4, gradually pour the cream into the chopped eggs. Add salt and pepper to taste with the mustard, then gradually stir in the oil. Add the chopped herbs with the vinegar and scrape into a serving bowl. Cover and leave in the refrigerator for 30 minutes.

3 Meanwhile, cook the new potatoes in lightly salted boiling water until tender. Drain, then stir the green sauce and pour over the hot new potatoes.

PISSALADIÈRE
A speciality of Nice, this French version of pizza can be made with either a bread dough, as here, or a pastry base and can be served hot or cold as just a snack or lunch.

SERVES 6

Preparation time: 20 minutes plus 1 hour rising time

Cooking time: 45 minutes

Attachments used

500 g plain flour

1 packet (7 g) active dry yeast

$^1/_2$ tsp salt

225 ml/1 cup warm water

600 g onions

4 Tbsp olive oil

2 tsp herbes de Provence

30 anchovy fillets in oil

20 black olives, stoned and halved

1 Put the flour, yeast and salt in the mixer bowl. With the dough hook, on speed 2, gradually add the warm water until a soft dough forms. Roll the dough out on a lightly floured surface to a round, 8 mm in thickness.

2 Fold the edge of the round back on itself to form a raised edge. Transfer the dough to a baking sheet covered in greaseproof paper and leave in a warm, draught-free place to rise for 1 hour.

3 Meanwhile, using the rotary slicer/shredder, with the slicing drum attached, on speed 4, slice the onions. Heat the olive oil in a saucepan and cook the onions with 1 teaspoon of the herbes de Provence over a medium heat until the onions are translucent. Transfer to a plate and leave to cool.

4 Preheat the oven to 200°C/Gas Mark 6. Once the dough has risen, sprinkle the onion mixture and the remaining herbs over the surface. Arrange the anchovies on top, crossing them to make a diamond pattern. Place a piece of olive inside each diamond. Cook for 10 minutes then reduce the oven temperature to 190°C/Gas Mark 5. Cook for a further 20 to 25 minutes until cooked through.

TORTA PASQUALINA (Savoury Easter tart) This unusual speciality from Genoa used to be made mainly at Easter and

takes a bit of effort. To make it easier, you could replace the home-made pastry with frozen puff pastry.

SERVES 10

Preparation time: 1 hour plus 1 hour resting time

Cooking time: 1 hour 20 minutes

Attachments used

For the pastry

500 g plain flour

Pinch of salt

2 Tbsp olive oil

250–300 ml/1^1/$_4$ cups water

For the filling

1 kg fresh spinach, tough stems removed

Salt and freshly ground black pepper

1–2 Tbsp chopped fresh marjoram

1 large dry bread roll, crusts removed

About 100 ml/^{1}/$_2$ cup milk

80 g Parmesan cheese

8 medium eggs

500 g ricotta cheese

5–6 Tbsp olive oil

50 g butter

1 Preheat the oven to 200°C/Gas Mark 6 and brush a 26-cm springform tin with a little oil. Sieve the flour with the salt into the mixer bowl. Using the dough hook, on speed 1, pour in the olive oil, then slowly pour in sufficient water to bring the mixture together until it forms a smooth but not sticky dough. Continue to knead the mixture with the dough hook on speed 2 for about 5 minutes until really smooth and pliable. Divide into 12 pieces, shape into balls and place on a lightly floured tea towel. Cover with a damp tea towel and leave to rest for 1 hour.

2 Meanwhile, prepare the filling. Place the spinach in a large saucepan and cook until just wilted with only the water left clinging to the leaves, adding a little salt. Drain thoroughly, squeezing out any excess liquid, then finely chop, season with salt and pepper to taste, and add the marjoram.

3 Cut the bread roll into small pieces and soak in the milk. Attach the rotary slicer/shredder fitted with the fine shredding drum, and grate the Parmesan cheese into the mixer bowl, on speed 4. Place in a separate bowl.

4 Break two of the eggs into the mixer bowl and, with the flat beater on speed 4, beat the eggs until blended, then beat in 2 tablespoons of the Parmesan cheese. Squeeze out any excess moisture from the bread roll and beat into the egg mixture. Add the ricotta cheese and beat on speed 2 until well blended, then beat in the chopped spinach.

5 Roll out one of the balls of pastry on a lightly floured surface, carefully stretching the pastry by hand in all directions like strudel pastry to make it as thin as possible. Arrange the pastry in the base of the oiled tin so that the pastry overhangs the edge by about 1 cm. Lightly brush with oil. Continue this for five further balls of pastry, brushing each layer with oil.

6 Spread the prepared filling on top of the six layers of pastry, smooth the top and brush with a little more oil. Using the back of a spoon, make six evenly spaced indentations in the filling and place a small pat of butter in each. Break an egg into each of the indentations, taking care not to break the yolks. Season with salt and pepper and sprinkle with the remaining Parmesan cheese.

7 Roll out the remaining balls of pastry and arrange on top, brushing each layer with oil as for the base. Place the remaining butter in small pieces round the edge of the pastry. Roll the overhanging pastry inwards over the butter and press down.

8 Brush the top with a little oil and carefully pierce in two to three places so that the steam can escape, then bake in the oven for 1 hour 15 minutes or until golden brown. Serve warm or cold.

PETITS LÉGUMES FARCIS (Little stuffed vegetables) This Provençal dish makes use of whatever is in season

– try stuffing small red, yellow or green peppers or courgettes. It can be eaten hot or cold for a simple summer lunch.

SERVES 4

Preparation time: 25 minutes

Cooking time: 40 minutes

Attachments used

4 large onions

4 large tomatoes

100 g bacon, diced

300 g cooked pork

1 Tbsp chopped fresh parsley

Salt and freshly ground black pepper

3 Tbsp crème fraîche

1 egg yolk

2 Tbsp olive oil

1 Preheat the oven to 180ºC/Gas Mark 4. Peel the onions, cut off a lid from each one and place them all in salted boiling water for 10 minutes. Drain and scoop out the insides, and chop finely, using the rotary slicer/shredder fitted with the fine shredding drum.

2 Cut lids off the tomatoes and scoop out the insides. Dust the insides of the tomatoes with salt and place upside down on kitchen paper.

3 Fry the bacon for 3 minutes. Add the chopped onion and sauté for 3 minutes.

4 Dice the cooked pork and mix with the parsley, bacon and onion and some seasoning. Pass the mixture through the food grinder fitted with the coarse grinding plate, on speed 4, then add the crème fraîche and egg yolk and, using the flat beater, mix in well.

5 Spoon the filling into the vegetables and replace the lids. Place in a roasting pan with a little water in the bottom and drizzle with the olive oil. Cook in the oven for 35 minutes, basting occasionally.

CAROTTES VICHY (Vichy carrots) A dish of slow-cooked glazed carrots, which were originally cooked in Vichy mineral water

from the Bourbonnais area of France, also famous for its root vegetables.

SERVES 4

Preparation time: 5 minutes

Cooking time: 1 hour

Attachments used

450 g carrots

1 large onion

2–4 cloves garlic

1 bouquet garni (thyme, rosemary and parsley)

1 Tbsp butter

1 tsp caster sugar

Salt and freshly ground black pepper

125 ml/^{1}/$_2$ cup water

1 Tbsp chopped fresh parsley

1   Preheat the oven to 180ºC/Gas Mark 4. Using the rotary slicer/shredder, with the slicing drum attached, on speed 4, slice the carrots, onion and garlic, and place in an ovenproof dish.

2   Add the remaining ingredients, except for the parsley, cover and cook in the oven for 1 hour or until the carrots are tender. Sprinkle with the chopped parsley and serve immediately.

The rotary slicer/shredder can slice, shred or grate straight into the mixer bowl, an oven dish or saucepan. To speed things up, do all your chopping before you start – you can even switch from one drum to another without removing the attachment from the KitchenAid mixer.

BRAISED RED CABBAGE
In this German cabbage dish, extra sweetness comes from the apple and apple juice.

If you want a less sweet dish, replace the juice with more red wine or water.

SERVES 4 TO 6

Preparation time: 10 minutes

Cooking time: 1 hour 30 minutes

Attachments used

1 onion

1 large cooking apple, peeled and cored

125 ml/$^1/_2$ cup balsamic vinegar

25 g caster sugar

80 g butter

100 ml/$^1/_2$ cup red wine

125 ml/$^1/_2$ cup apple juice

4 juniper berries, lightly crushed

Salt and freshly ground black pepper

500 g red cabbage, outer leaves and hard central core discarded

1   Using the rotary slicer/shredder, with the slicing drum attached, on speed 4, slice the onion and apple into the bowl, then transfer to a heavy based saucepan. Add the remaining ingredients, except for the cabbage, and bring to the boil.

2   Meanwhile slice the red cabbage through the slicing drum, on speed 4, and wash in plenty of cold water. Drain thoroughly, add to the saucepan and return to the boil.

3   Cover with the lid and reduce to a simmer, then cook for about 1 hour 30 minutes. While the cabbage cooks, take care not to allow the liquid to evaporate completely – top up with apple juice or red wine and water mixed and turn the heat down if necessary. Cook until tender, stirring frequently, and serve hot with meats or stews.

BRAISED CELERY HEARTS
A simple dish to prepare as a perfect accompaniment to white fish, celery hearts bring the flavour of French bistros to the table. If your celery is on the large side, break off the stalks, remove the strings with a vegetable peeler and cut them into 5-cm lengths.

SERVES 4

Preparation time: 10 minutes

Cooking time: 45 minutes

Attachments used

1 carrot, peeled

1 onion, peeled

5 or 6 celery hearts

50 g butter

Salt and freshly ground black pepper

500 ml/2 cups vegetable or chicken stock

1 bouquet garni

1   Using the rotary slicer/shredder, with the coarse shredding drum attached, on speed 4, slice the carrot and onion and chop into a bowl.

2   Remove the outer stalks of the celery to reveal the hearts. Keep them whole, removing just the leaves and the woody parts.

3   Rinse the celery hearts and blanch them for 5 minutes in well-salted boiling water. Drain and cool immediately in cold water.

4   Preheat the oven to 180 °C/Gas Mark 4. Melt the butter in a saucepan over low heat. Add the carrot and onion and fry them gently, without browning, until they are soft. Add the celery, season, and cover with the stock. Add the bouquet garni, cover, and place in the oven. After 20 minutes, turn the celery and return to the oven for a further 20 minutes. Serve hot.

SERVIETTENKNÖDEL (Napkin dumplings) A simple Central European dumpling made from tiny bits of bread soaked in

milk and steamed with onion. Serve as a side dish with winter stews, country soups or braised red cabbage (see page 88).

SERVES 4

Preparation time: 20 minutes plus 30 minutes soaking time

Cooking time: 1 hour 20 minutes

Attachments used

6 crusty bread rolls (total weight about 250 g)

2 eggs

120 ml/$^{1}/_{2}$ cup milk

$^{1}/_{4}$ tsp salt

1 onion, cut into 8 wedges

50 g butter

Handful fresh parsley leaves, finely chopped

Pinch of grated nutmeg

Freshly ground black pepper

1   Preheat the oven to 100°C/Gas Mark $^{1}/_{4}$. Cut the bread rolls into 1 cm cubes or tear into tiny pieces. Put on a baking sheet and bake for 20 minutes, turning occasionally until dry. Tip them into a large bowl.

2   Whisk the eggs, milk and salt together. Slowly pour the mixture over the bread and gently stir to ensure the pieces are evenly coated.

3   Using the rotary slicer/shredder with the coarse shredding drum attached, on speed 4, grate the onion into the bowl and set aside.

4   Melt the butter in a frying pan and gently cook the onion for 10 to 15 minutes until soft. Add the parsley and cook for another minute. Remove from the heat and allow to cool for a few minutes, then add to the bread. Season with nutmeg and pepper and mix thoroughly, then cover and leave in a cool place for at least 30 minutes to soak.

5   Shape the mixture into a roll, about 10 cm long. Place it on a clean, wet tea towel and roll up the cloth to enclose the mixture like a large sausage. Leave a little room at the ends for the dumpling to expand, then tie up in the middle and both ends with string.

6   Slide a wooden spoon through the string and hang the dumpling over a pot of boiling lightly salted water, covering just over half of the dumpling. Cover with a lid and gently simmer for 30 minutes. Carefully turn the dumpling over, so that the top side is now in the water, and cook for a further 25 minutes.

7   Remove from the water and leave it to stand for 5 minutes. To serve, carefully unwrap the dumpling and cut it into thick slices.

GRATIN DAUPHINOIS

A French dish of potatoes in cream, baked until a golden crust forms. To make boulangère potatoes, substitute a quarter of the potatoes for sliced onions, cover with vegetable stock, then dot with butter before baking.

SERVES 6

Preparation time: 15 minutes

Cooking time: 1 hour 15 minutes

Attachments used

1 kg potatoes

Butter

2 cloves garlic, chopped

50 g gruyère

Salt and freshly ground black pepper

100 ml/$^1/_2$ cup double cream

400 ml/2 cups milk

1 Preheat the oven to 180°C/Gas Mark 4. With the slicing drum on the rotary slicer/shredder, on speed 4, slice the potatoes. Using the fine shredding drum, grate the gruyère.

2 Generously butter an ovenproof dish. Put the potatoes into the dish and tuck pieces of garlic and grated gruyère in amongst them. Season well. Mix the cream and milk together and pour over the potatoes – it should come just to the top of the potatoes. Sprinkle gruyère over the top.

3 Cover with foil, and bake in the oven for about 1 hour 15 minutes, until the potatoes are tender. Remove the foil cover for the last 15 minutes of cooking time, to form a golden-brown crust.

ROSTI WITH APPLE SAUCE
Hot potato pancakes make a great accompaniment to sausages and roasted or grilled meats, or they can be served on their own as a snack with a spoonful of apple sauce.

SERVES 6

Preparation time: 10 minutes

Cooking time: 20 minutes

Attachments used

6 large waxy potatoes

1 onion, cut into wedges

1 clove garlic (optional)

4 Tbsp plain flour

2 eggs, beaten

Salt and freshly ground black pepper

50 g unsalted butter

4 Tbsp oil

For the apple sauce

225 g tart apples, peeled and cored

225 g eating apples, peeled and cored

20 g caster sugar

2 Tbsp water

1 Place a sieve over the mixer bowl. Using the rotary slicer/shredder with the coarse shredding drum attached, on speed 4, grate the potatoes into the sieve. Press as much liquid out of the grated potatoes as possible. Discard the liquid and tip the potatoes into the bowl.

2 Change to the medium shredding drum and, still on speed 4, grate the onion and garlic into the bowl. Sprinkle over the flour, then add the eggs. Season with salt and pepper and mix well.

3 To make the apple sauce, use the slicing drum to slice the apples into a saucepan. Add the sugar and water. Cover and simmer for 15 minutes. Stir occasionally during cooking. Beat with a fork and set aside.

4 Heat half the butter and half the oil together in a large frying pan, then add large spoonfuls of the potato mixture to form rounds. Flatten the pancakes with the back of a dampened spoon.

5 Fry the pancakes over a medium heat until dark golden brown and crisp, then turn over and cook on the other side. Drain on kitchen paper and keep warm while cooking the rest of the pancakes, adding more butter and oil to the pan when needed. Serve hot with the apple sauce.

SWEET CUCUMBER PICKLE
This sweet pickle can be stuffed into wholegrain sandwiches with cheese or carved leg ham and salad, or served on the side with hamburgers or hot dogs.

MAKES 600 ML/2^1/$_2$ CUPS

Preparation time: 20 minutes plus 2 hours standing time

Cooking time: 25 minutes

Attachments used

3 large onions

3 large cucumbers, unpeeled

50 g fine sea salt

450 g caster sugar

600 ml/2^1/$_2$ cups white wine vinegar

1 Tbsp mustard seeds

1   With the slicing drum on the rotary slicer/shredder, on speed 4, slice the onions and the cucumbers.

2   In a large colander layer the vegetables, sprinkling the salt between the layers. Place a plate on top and press down with a heavy weight. Leave for at least 2 hours, then squeeze out as much of the remaining liquid as possible.

3   In a large pan, stir the sugar into the vinegar with the mustard seeds until the sugar has dissolved completely. Bring slowly to the boil.

4   Add the drained vegetables and again bring to the boil. Simmer, uncovered, for 1 minute. Remove from the heat and drain the vegetables, reserving the liquid, then spoon into hot, sterilized jars. Return the liquid to the pan and boil for a further 15 minutes, uncovered, then pour over the onion and cucumber in the jars. Seal when completely cold.

PEACH CHUTNEY
Similar to India's mango chutney, this peach chutney is a wonderful accompaniment to spicy curries, as well as a great partner for cold meats or bread and cheese.

MAKES 2.5 LITRES/5 CUPS

Preparation time: 20 minutes

Cooking time: 2 hours

Attachments used

12 firm peaches, halved and stoned

3 red peppers, deseeded and quartered

1 large onion, halved

175 ml/^{3}/$_4$ cup cider vinegar

150 g sugar

^{1}/$_2$ clove garlic, crushed

^{1}/$_2$ tsp salt

85 g raisins

^{1}/$_2$ navel orange, peeled, deseeded and quartered

^{1}/$_2$ lemon, peeled, deseeded and quartered

50 g chopped crystallized ginger

^{1}/$_2$ tsp ground ginger

1 With the slicing drum on the rotary slicer/shredder, on speed 4, slice the peaches, peppers and onion thickly and set aside.

2 Heat 125 ml/^{1}/$_2$ cup of the vinegar and the sugar in a 5-litre pot over a medium heat. Bring the mixture to the boil, then reduce the heat and simmer for 10 minutes.

3 Add the peach, pepper, onion, garlic, salt and raisins to the pot. Simmer, stirring frequently, for 10 minutes.

4 Using the food grinder, with the coarse grinding plate attached, on speed 4, grind the orange and lemon. Add the pulped fruit and crystallized ginger to the pot and simmer for 30 minutes, stirring occasionally.

5 Add the remaining vinegar and ground ginger to the mixture. Simmer for 1 hour or until thick, stirring occasionally. Ladle the mixture into hot, sterilized jars and seal them. Place in a saucepan of boiling water and simmer for 15 minutes. Remove the jars from the bath, then cool them and check the seals.

COURGETTE AND TOMATO SAUTE
You can, if preferred, use marrow or any other squash for this recipe. If using squashes such as acorn or butternut squash, ensure that they are young and tender when you buy them.

SERVES 4

Preparation time: 10 minutes

Cooking time: 20 minutes

Attachments used

1 onion

1–2 cloves garlic

450 g courgettes

25 g unsalted butter

400-g can chopped tomatoes

Salt and freshly ground black pepper

1 Tbsp chopped fresh oregano

100 g feta cheese, diced (optional)

1 With the slicing drum on the rotary slicer/shredder, on speed 4, slice the onion, garlic and courgettes separately. Heat the butter in a large frying pan, then sauté the onion and garlic for 3 minutes. Add the courgettes and continue to sauté for 2 minutes.

2 Add the tomatoes, with seasoning to taste, and the chopped oregano and bring to the boil, stirring occasionally. Reduce the heat, cover with either a lid or tinfoil and simmer for 10 to 15 minutes or until the vegetables are tender. Adjust the seasoning and add the cheese if using.

COURGETTES WITH GARLIC
A classic partnership of courgettes with a little garlic. Instead of grating the courgettes, you could use the slicing drum to slice them thinly, then cook in the same way.

SERVES 2

Preparation time: 10 minutes

Cooking time: 10 minutes

Attachments used

2 medium or 4 small courgettes

2 cloves garlic, finely chopped

Olive oil

Salt and freshly ground black pepper

1 Grate the courgettes, using the coarse shredding drum on the rotary slicer/shredder, on speed 4.

2 Put the garlic in a pan in which a small quantity of olive oil has been heated. When the garlic starts to give off its aroma, but before it turns brown, tip in the courgettes.

3 Cook over a moderate heat for 5 to 10 minutes, until the courgettes are just cooked. Season and serve.

LEEK AND COURGETTE QUICHE
A vegetarian quiche made with a classic shortcrust pastry that combines lard and butter for both texture and flavour. Choose small leeks with tender green tops as these are the sweetest when cooked.

SERVES 4 TO 6

Preparation time: 30 minutes,
            plus 30 minutes chilling

Cooking time: 45 minutes

Attachments used

For the pastry

225 g plain flour

Pinch of salt

50 g butter

20 g lard

120 ml/^{1}/$_2$ cup iced water

For the filling

50 g butter

3 leeks, sliced

1 courgette, sliced

1 clove garlic, crushed

4 large eggs

2 Tbsp plain yoghurt

120 ml/^{1}/$_2$ cup milk

100 g gruyère or mature Cheddar cheese, grated

Salt and freshly ground black pepper

1 Preheat the oven to 190°C/Gas Mark 5. Sieve the flour and salt into the mixer bowl. Cut the butter and lard into cubes and add to the flour. Using the flat beater, on speed 2, beat until well blended. Add enough iced water to make a smooth dough, then shape into a ball, wrap in clingfilm and chill in the refrigerator for 30 minutes.

2 To make the filling, heat the butter in a pan. Gently fry the leek, courgette and garlic until soft. Remove from the heat.

3 Mix the eggs, yoghurt, milk, cheese and some salt and pepper thoroughly in a bowl.

4 Roll out the dough thinly and line a 20-cm baking tin. Add the leek and courgette filling and pour in the cheese mixture. Smooth it over on top.

5 Bake in the oven for about 45 minutes until the quiche is firm and golden brown. Garnish with salad leaves and serve hot or cold.

SPINACH AND CHEESE SOUFFLÉ

French soufflés are not as difficult to make as their reputation implies, in fact the hardest part can be ensuring that everyone is assembled when the soufflé is brought to the table so they can appreciate how well it has risen.

SERVES 4

Preparation time: 45 minutes

Cooking time: 50 minutes

Attachments used

300 g fresh spinach, washed thoroughly

100 g mature Cheddar cheese

50 g unsalted butter

50 g plain flour

200 ml/1 cup warm milk

4 medium eggs, separated

1 tsp Dijon mustard

Salt and freshly ground black pepper

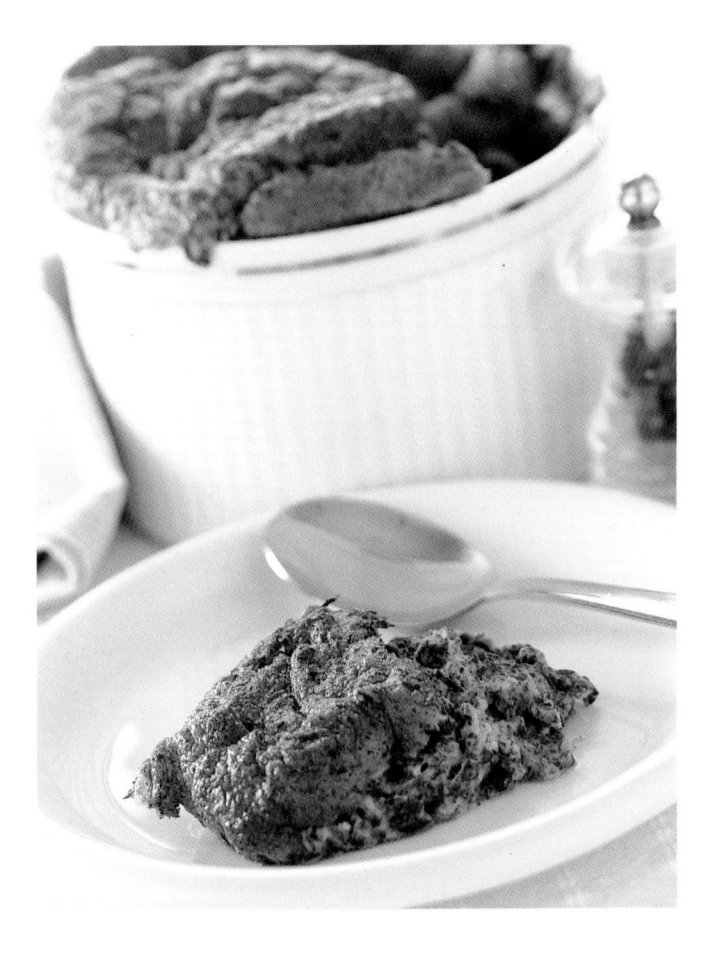

1 Preheat the oven to 180ºC/Gas Mark 4. Lightly butter a 1.3 litre soufflé dish. Place a baking sheet in the oven to heat. Place the spinach, with just the water clinging to the leaves, into a saucepan and cook for 3 to 4 minutes or until wilted. Drain thoroughly and chop finely, then place in kitchen paper and squeeze out any excess moisture.

2 With the coarse shredding drum on the rotary slicer/shredder, on speed 4, grate the cheese.

3 Melt the butter in a saucepan and stir in the flour, cook over a gentle heat for 2 minutes, then draw the pan off the heat and gradually stir in the warm milk. Return to the heat and stir for 2 minutes, or until the mixture thickens and coats the back of the spoon. Remove from the heat and place in the mixer bowl.

4 Cool slightly, then with the flat beater, at speed 6, beat in the egg yolks one at a time, beating well between each addition. When all the egg yolks have been added, stir in the spinach and all but 1 tablespoon of the cheese, along with the mustard and some seasoning. Stir until the cheese has melted. Pour into another bowl.

5 Clean the mixer bowl and dry thoroughly, then add the egg whites and using the wire whip, on speed 10, whisk until stiff and standing in peaks. Stir 1 tablespoon into the cheese mixture, then gently stir in the remaining egg whites.

6 Spoon the mixture into the prepared dish, place on the hot baking sheet and cook undisturbed in the oven for 50 minutes, or until well risen and golden brown. Serve immediately.

BREADS

GRANARY AND WALNUT BREAD
Granary flour is a mixture of white, wholemeal and rye flours blended with malted grains. The flour gives a nutty taste that complements the walnuts in this country bread.

MAKES 2 LOAVES

Preparation time: 15 minutes plus standing time

Cooking time: 40 minutes

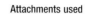

Attachments used

1 kg granary flour

2 tsp salt

1 packet (7 g) active dry yeast

75 g walnuts, roughly chopped

2 Tbsp oil

About 600 ml/2^1/$_2$ cups tepid water

1 Preheat the oven to 220°C/Gas Mark 7. Place the flour, salt, yeast and nuts into the mixer bowl. Using the flat beater, on speed 2, mix the dry ingredients for a few seconds.

2 Change to the dough hook and, on speed 2 again, gradually add the oil and the tepid water. If the mixture looks at all dry, add a little more water until it looks moist. Knead for about 1 minute only on this speed. Place in a greased bowl, turning the dough over once to grease the top. Cover and leave to rise in a warm, draught-free place for about 1 hour, or until doubled in bulk.

3 Knead well again, adding a little extra flour if the dough seems too sticky. The machine may be stopped once or twice and the dough pulled away from hook. Divide into two and place in two greased 1-kg loaf tins. Cover and leave to rise in a warm place, free from draughts, for about 1 hour, or until risen well above the tops of the tins.

4 Bake in the oven for 10 minutes, then reduce the heat to 200°C/Gas Mark 6 for another 30 minutes. The loaves are cooked when, turned out of their tins, they sound hollow if tapped on the base. Cool on a wire rack.

When making bread add the liquids gradually so they do not form a pool around the dough hook and slow down the mixing process.

The KitchenAid mixer will really start to knead the bread when the dough begins to cling to the dough hook, and you can then continue kneading until the dough is smooth.

PAIN DE CAMPAGNE (Country bread) A coarse French loaf made from a mixture of buckwheat, rye and white flours.

This everyday bread keeps well and makes great toast.

MAKES 2 SMALL LOAVES

Preparation time: 15 minutes plus 1 hour 45 minutes rising time

Cooking time: 40 minutes

Attachments used

200 g buckwheat flour

200 g rye flour

375 g strong white bread flour

2 tsp salt

1 packet (7 g) active dry yeast

1 Tbsp clear honey

250 ml/1 cup warm water

30 g melted butter

150 ml/$^2/_3$ cup strong dark beer

1 Put the flours, salt and yeast in the mixer bowl and blend with the dough hook on speed 1 for a few seconds.

2 Stir the honey into the water until mixed together, then add the melted butter and beer and mix again.

3 Using the dough hook on speed 2, gradually add the beer mixture to the bowl and blend to a smooth dough. Continue kneading with the dough hook on speed 2 for 5 to 6 more minutes, until the dough is smooth and elastic.

4 Cover the bowl with clingfilm and leave the dough to rise in a warm, draught-free place for about an hour, or until doubled in bulk.

5 Punch the dough down, then divide into two and shape each half into a round loaf. Transfer to a greased baking sheet, cover with oiled clingfilm and leave to rise for a further 45 minutes, or until doubled in size.

6 Meanwhile, preheat the oven to 220°C/Gas Mark 7. Lightly dust the tops of the loaves with flour, then slash in a criss-cross pattern with a sharp knife.

7 Bake for 10 minutes, then lower the heat to 200°C/Gas Mark 6 and bake for a further 25 to 30 minutes, until the loaves are risen and sound hollow when tapped underneath.

TOMATO AND OLIVE OIL BREAD
Similar in preparation to traditional focaccia, yet much faster, this olive oil bread is enlivened with sweet tomatoes and garlic. It's delicious served with fresh goat's cheese and a salad.

MAKES 1 LARGE LOAF

Preparation time: 30 minutes plus 2 hours 20 minutes rising time

Cooking time: 30 minutes

Attachments used

500 g strong white bread flour

1 Tbsp salt

1 packet (7 g) active dry yeast

100 ml/$1/2$ cup olive oil

300 ml/$1^1/2$ cups lukewarm water

12 cherry tomatoes, halved

1 to 2 cloves garlic, very finely sliced

Olive oil and coarse sea salt, for topping

1 Blend the flour, salt and yeast together on speed 2 using the dough hook, then add the olive oil and most of the water. Mix, and knead thoroughly, still on speed 2, adding enough water to make a soft but manageable dough. The kneading will take about 5 to 6 minutes.

2 Scrape the dough off the hook back into the bowl. Cover with clingfilm and leave in a warm, draught-free place for two hours until well risen.

3 Knead the dough again, with the dough hook on speed 2, until the dough returns to its original size. Turn out onto a lightly floured surface.

4 Generously oil a small rectangular roasting tin, about 20 x 25 cm. Divide the dough in half and roll out one piece to roughly fit the base of the tin, stretching it into the corners. Cover with the halved tomatoes and garlic and season lightly with salt and pepper. Roll out the remaining dough and place it over the tomatoes. Cover the pan with clingfilm and leave in a warm, draught-free place again for about 20 minutes, until just starting to rise.

5 Preheat the oven to 220°C/Gas Mark 7. Carefully make indentations all over the dough with your fingertips to seal the two halves together and stop the dough from rising too much. Drizzle with a little olive oil and sprinkle with coarse sea salt, then bake for 25 to 30 minutes until golden brown. Cool on a wire rack before serving.

PITTA BREAD
This Middle-Eastern flatbread can be cooked in the oven or on a griddle or open fire. It puffs up to leave a pocket that can be stuffed with a sandwich filling or torn open to scoop up a spicy dip.

MAKES 6 PITTA BREADS

Preparation time: 30 minutes plus 2 hours standing time

Cooking time: 30 minutes

Attachments used

115 g wholewheat flour

385 g plain flour

1 Tbsp sugar

2 tsp salt

1 packet (7 g) active dry yeast

450 ml/2 cups very warm water

1 Tbsp olive oil

1 Mix the flours together and place 450 g of this mixture in the mixer bowl, with the sugar, salt and yeast. Using the dough hook, on speed 2, mix for 15 seconds. Gradually add the warm water and olive oil and mix for 1 minute. Continuing on speed 2, add the remaining flour mixture, 50 g at a time, until the dough cleans the sides of the bowl. Knead on speed 2 for 2 minutes longer, or until the dough is smooth and elastic.

2 Cover and leave to rise in a warm, draught-free place for about 1 hour, or until doubled in bulk. Preheat the oven to 260°C/Gas Mark 9.

3 Punch the dough down and divide into six equal pieces. Roll each piece into an 18-cm circle, and place on foil to rise, uncovered, at room temperature for 1 hour. Bake for 5 to 6 minutes. Cool on a wire rack.

SOURDOUGH

Sourdough is made from a starter that can be refrigerated and used as needed. Stir 125 ml/¹/₂ cup water and 125 g strong white bread flour into the remaining starter from the recipe below and leave to ferment at room temperature for 12 to 24 hours before refrigerating.

MAKES 1 LOAF

Preparation time: 20 minutes plus 2 hours rising and 2 to 3 days fermenting time

Cooking time: 40 minutes

Attachments used

For the starter

250 g strong white bread flour

1 packet (7 g) active dry yeast

300 ml/1¹/₄ cups water

For the dough

375 g strong white bread flour

1¹/₂ tsp salt

1 tsp active dry yeast

175 ml/³/₄ cup tepid water

1 To make the starter, sieve the flour into the mixer bowl and stir in the yeast. Add the water and stir together with the flat beater. Pour into a bowl, loosely cover and keep in a warm draught-free place. The mixture is ready to use when it has a pleasant sour smell, between 2 and 3 days. Stir it twice daily.

2 To make the dough, sieve the flour and salt into the mixer bowl and stir in the yeast. Measure 250 ml/1 cup of the starter into a jug, reserving the remaining starter, then stir in the tepid water. Using the dough hook, on speed 1, gradually add the starter mixture and blend to a smooth dough. Continue kneading on speed 2 for another 3 minutes, until smooth and elastic.

3 Cover the bowl with clingfilm and leave the dough to rise in a warm draught-free place for about an hour, until doubled in size. Knock back, then leave to rest for 10 minutes.

4 Shape the dough into a round or long oval shape and place on a greased baking sheet. Cover with oiled clingfilm and leave to rise in a warm draught-free place for about an hour, or until doubled in size.

5 Place a tray of water on the bottom shelf of the oven, then preheat the oven to 220°C/Gas Mark 7. Lightly dust the loaf with flour, then cut three parallel slashes about 5 mm deep across the top of the loaf, and three more slashes in the opposite direction to make a criss-cross pattern.

6 Bake the loaf for 10 minutes, then reduce the heat to 200°C/Gas Mark 6 and bake for a further 30 minutes, or until golden and hollow-sounding when tapped on the bottom. Leave to cool on a wire rack.

CHALLAH This is a Jewish plaited egg bread, sprinkled with poppy or sesame seeds. The bread has a religious significance and two loaves are traditionally served at every meal on the Jewish sabbath and at religious festivals.

MAKES 2 LOAVES

Preparation time: 30 minutes plus 2 hours standing time

Cooking time: 35 minutes

Attachments used

500–625 g plain flour

2 Tbsp sugar

1$^1/_2$ tsp salt

1 packet (7 g) active dry yeast

75 g butter or margarine, melted

225 ml/1 cup very warm water

3 eggs

1 egg, separated

1 tsp cold water

1 tsp poppy seeds

1 Preheat the oven to 200ºC/Gas Mark 6. Place 450 g of the flour in the mixer bowl, with the sugar, salt and yeast, and using the dough hook, mix for 15 seconds on speed 2. Combine the butter and water, gradually add to the bowl and mix for 1 minute. Add the three eggs and the egg white and mix for 1 minute more. Add the remaining flour, 50 g at a time, until the dough clings to the hook and cleans the sides of the bowl. Knead on speed 2 for 2 minutes longer, or until the dough is smooth and elastic.

2 Place in a greased bowl, turning the dough over once to grease the top. Cover and leave to rise in a warm place, free from draughts, for about 1 hour, or until doubled in bulk.

3 Punch the dough down and divide into six equal pieces. Roll each piece into a 35-cm rope. Plait three ropes together, tucking the ends under, and place on a greased baking sheet. Repeat with the remaining ropes. Cover and leave to rise in a warm place, free from draughts, for about 1 hour, or until doubled in bulk.

4 Beat the egg yolk and cold water together. Brush the loaves with glaze and sprinkle with the poppy seeds. Bake in the oven for 30 to 35 minutes. Remove from the baking sheets immediately and cool on a wire rack.

SODA BREAD This is an Irish quick bread, using bicarbonate of soda and sour milk instead of yeast and not requiring any rising time. Enjoy this bread at its best by eating it the day it is made.

MAKES 1 LOAF

Preparation time: 10 minutes

Cooking time: 30 minutes

Attachments used

450 g plain flour

1 level tsp salt

1 level tsp bicarbonate of soda

350–375 ml/1$^1/_2$ cups buttermilk

1 Preheat the oven to 230ºC/Gas Mark 8. Sieve the dry ingredients into the mixer bowl and, using the flat beater on speed 2, gradually add the buttermilk (you may not need it all) until it forms a dough. Switch to the dough hook and, on speed 2, knead until you have a soft but not sticky dough.

2 On a greased baking sheet, pat the dough into a round about 2.5 cm thick. Bake in the oven for 15 minutes, then reduce the heat to 200ºC/Gas Mark 6 and bake for a further 15 minutes.

3 To test that it is done, tap the bottom of the loaf – it should sound hollow. Cool on a wire rack and eat the same day.

HUNSRÜCKER BAUERENBROT (Rye and wheat bread) Spelt is an ancestor of wheat and

contains more protein, B-vitamins and iron but less gluten, resulting in a close-textured moist bread. If you can't find it, use more wholemeal flour instead.

This German loaf is made with a sourdough starter that takes a few days to ferment if making from scratch.

MAKES 2 LOAVES

Preparation time: 15 minutes plus 2 hours 15 minutes rising time

Cooking time: 40 minutes

Attachments used

350 g strong wholemeal flour

200 g rye flour

100 g spelt flour

1 Tbsp salt

1 packet (7 g) active dry yeast

120 ml/^{1}/$_2$ cup starter dough (page 102)

400 ml/1^2/$_3$ cups warm water

1 Put the flours, salt and yeast in the mixer bowl and mix for a few seconds with the dough hook on speed 1. Stir the starter dough and warm water together in a jug and, using the dough hook on speed 2, gradually add to the dry ingredients and blend to a smooth dough. Continue kneading for 5 to 6 minutes or until smooth and elastic.

2 Cover the bowl with clingfilm and leave the dough to rise in a warm, draught-free place for about 1^1/$_2$ hours, or until doubled in bulk.

3 Punch the dough down, divide in half and shape each one into an oblong. Place on a lightly oiled baking sheet, cover loosely with oiled clingfilm and leave to rise for about 45 minutes.

4 Preheat the oven to 220°C/Gas Mark 7. Brush the tops of the loaves with lukewarm water and make a few diagonal slashes with a sharp knife. Bake for 35 to 40 minutes until the loaves are risen and browned. To test whether the loaves are cooked, tap them on the base – they should sound hollow. Leave in the tins for 10 minutes, then transfer to a wire rack to cool.

Using the grain mill to make your own flours for this bread will produce a wonderfully fresh loaf, with a rougher, more country-style texture. Use just a little less wheat and rye berries than the amount of flour stated, set the grain mill to click 3 and grind into the mixer bowl on speed 10.

FOCACCIA An Italian flatbread, traditionally toasted over an open fire and topped with olive oil and coarse salt. There are many variations, and this one is made with mashed potatoes and covered with tomatoes and oregano.

SERVES 12

Preparation time: 10 minutes plus 3 hours proving time

Cooking time: 30 minutes

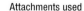

Attachments used

500 g strong white bread flour

500 g cooked and mashed potatoes (page 80)

4 Tbsp olive oil

1 packet (7 g) active dry yeast

2 eggs

1 tsp salt

For the topping

150 ml/¹/₂ cup olive oil

15 small tomatoes, halved or quartered

2 Tbsp chopped fresh oregano or thyme

Pinch of salt

1 Preheat the oven to 180°C/Gas Mark 4. Put the flour, mashed potatoes, olive oil, yeast, eggs and salt into the mixer bowl. With the dough hook, mix the dough on speed 2 for 30 seconds. Increase to speed 4 and continue mixing until a smooth dough forms. Divide into two.

2 Lightly grease a two 20-cm round cake tins and shape the dough into the tin. Lightly cover the top and leave to rest for 3 hours until risen.

3 Brush the olive oil over the dough and arrange the tomato pieces on top. Sprinkle the oregano, or thyme, and salt on the tomatoes and cook in the oven for 30 minutes, covering lightly with foil halfway through cooking to prevent the topping from browning. Serve warm.

PRETZELS
The original bar snack, pretzels originated in Germany and Austria but are now just as popular in America. They should be salty and hard on the outside, but have a chewy interior.

MAKES 10 TO 12 PRETZELS

Preparation time: 15 minutes, plus 15 minutes standing time

Cooking time: 30 minutes

Attachments used

500 g plain flour
Pinch of salt
4 packets (28 g) active dry yeast
40 g sugar
75 g lard, softened and cut into flakes
125 ml/^{1}/$_2$ cup tepid milk
50 g plain flour, for dusting
125 ml/^{1}/$_2$ cup salted warm water, for brushing
1 Tbsp coarse salt, for sprinkling

1 Preheat the oven to 220ºC/Gas Mark 7. Put the flour, pinch of salt, yeast, sugar and the lard in the mixer bowl. Using the dough hook on speed 1, mix in the tepid milk until the mixture forms a dough. Cover and leave to rest in a warm, draught-free place for 15 minutes.

2 Using the dough hook on speed 1, knead again to make a supple but firm dough that is elastic and leaves the sides of the bowl clean.

3 Dust your hands with the flour and make 40-cm long rolls of dough, about 1-cm in diameter. Turn both ends of each roll inwards into a loose knot shape.

4 Place the pretzels on a greased baking sheet. Brush with the salted water and sprinkle them with salt, very gently pressing the salt grains into the dough.

5 Bake in the oven for 30 minutes, brushing the pretzels with the salted water twice again during baking so they are nice and crispy. Allow to cool, then store the pretzels in an airtight container.

CHAPATI

CHAPATI A circular flatbread made in India and Pakistan from a fine wholewheat chapati flour, called atta, and water. This version uses wholewheat flour. Chapatis are used to scoop up curries.

MAKES 12 CHAPATIS

Preparation time: 15 minutes plus 30 minutes standing time

Cooking time: 30 minutes

Attachments used

175 ml/ ³/₄ cup water
250 g wholemeal flour, sieved
Pinch of salt
Butter or oil, for brushing

1 In the mixer bowl, with the dough hook on speed 1, gradually add the water to the sieved flour and the salt to form a soft dough. It will be quite sticky. Knead for 4 to 5 minutes on speed 2. Cover with the plastic bowl cover and leave to rise in a warm, draught-free place for about 30 minutes.

2 Divide the dough into 12 pieces. Take one piece and roll into a ball, then flatten. Using a rolling pin and dusting well with flour, roll into a circle about 12 to 14 cm in diameter.

3 Shake off any excess flour and put it onto a preheated cast-iron flat griddle or frying pan. Cook on a low heat for 1 to 2 minutes. Turn the chapati over and cook on the other side.

4 Brush a little melted butter or some oil over the surface of the chapati and eat while fresh. Make the rest of the chapatis in the same way.

STOLLEN

These traditional sweet loaves are found all over northern Europe in the winter, although they originate in Germany. Tie the baked stollen with a ribbon to make a charming gift for friends at Christmas time.

MAKES 2 LOAVES

Preparation time: 2 hours plus 2 hours 30 minutes standing time

Cooking time: 30 minutes

Attachments used

1 packet (7 g) active dry yeast

1 tsp caster sugar

500 g plain flour

150 ml/⅔ cup lukewarm milk

Pinch of salt

3 Tbsp light brown sugar or light Muscovado sugar, if available

50 g butter, cut into slices

2 eggs, beaten

1 Tbsp rum

150 g mixed dried fruit

Grated rind of half a lemon

150 g marzipan or almond paste

Butter, for glazing

Icing sugar, for dredging

1 Stir the yeast, caster sugar, 125 g of the flour and the milk together in the mixer bowl, using the flat beater. Cover and leave in a warm place for at least an hour, until it starts to become frothy.

2 Add the remaining flour, salt, brown sugar, butter, most, but not all, of the beaten eggs and the rum and mix to a manageable dough with the dough hook on speed 4, adding a little extra milk if necessary. Knead thoroughly with the dough hook on speed 4 for 5 minutes, then cover and leave in a warm, draught-free place for an hour, or until doubled in bulk.

3 Knead the dough lightly, then gently work in the dried fruit and lemon rind using the dough hook on speed 4, do not overknead. Turn out onto a lightly floured surface and divide into two. Shape into ovals, about 1.5 cm thick.

4 Roll the marzipan into two even lengths to fit the length of the loaves. Press the rolling pin into the dough to make an indentation about one-third of the way from the bottom of each oval. Lay the marzipan in the marked places, then fold the dough over towards you, leaving the ends of the marzipan just showing if possible. Seal the edges with some of

the remaining beaten egg. Place the loaves on a lightly buttered baking tray, cover and leave to rise again for about 30 minutes.

5 Preheat the oven to 180°C/Gas Mark 4. Brush the dough with any remaining egg and bake for 30 minutes, or until golden brown.

6 Cool on a wire rack. Melt a little extra butter and brush over the cooled loaves and top with sieved icing sugar.

PANETTONE
This light and buttery cake-like bread from Milan is traditionally eaten over Christmas and Easter. Do not add more than the amount of flour specified or the panettone will be dry.

MAKES 1 LOAF

Preparation time: 40 minutes plus 2 hours standing time

Cooking time: 1 hour

Attachments used

1 packet (7 g) active dry yeast

225 ml/1 cup warm milk

450–500 g plain flour

1 tsp salt

85 g raisins

1 tsp grated lemon peel

95 g chopped citron or candied peel

55 g sugar

125 ml/$^1/_2$ cup vegetable oil

55 g butter, melted

4 egg yolks

1 egg white

1 Tbsp water

1 Preheat the oven to 180°C/Gas Mark 4. Dissolve the yeast in the warm milk. Place 350 g of the flour, the salt, raisins, lemon peel, citron and sugar in the mixer bowl. Using the dough hook, on speed 2, mix for 15 seconds. Add the oil and butter to the mixture.

2 On speed 2, gradually add the warm milk and yeast and the egg yolks to the mixer bowl and mix for 1 minute. Continuing on speed 2, add the remaining flour, 50 g at a time, until the dough clings to the hook and cleans the sides of the bowl. Knead on speed 2 for 2 minutes longer.

3 Place in a greased bowl, turning the dough over once to grease the top. Cover and leave to rise in a warm, draught-free place for about 1 hour, or until doubled in bulk.

4 Punch the dough down and shape into a ball. Place in a greased and floured 1.7-litre soufflé dish. Again, leave to rise, but this time uncovered, in a warm, draught-free place for a further hour, until doubled in bulk.

5 Cut two slashes with a sharp knife in a cross pattern on the top of the loaf. Beat the egg white and water together with a fork and brush the top of the loaf with this mixture. Bake the loaf in the oven for 55 to 60 minutes.

6 When cooked, remove the loaf from the baking dish immediately and allow to cool on a wire rack.

FLACHSWICKEL

(Sweet plaited rolls) Little German rolls, made with lots of butter, coated in icing sugar and plaited. Serve warm at breakfast time with home-made fruit jam or some honey.

MAKES 8

Preparation time: 15 minutes plus 1 hour rising time

Cooking time: 20 minutes

Attachments used

150 g butter

200 ml/²/₃ cup milk

500 g plain flour

1 packet (7 g) active dry yeast

2 Tbsp caster sugar

2 eggs

Pinch of salt

2 Tbsp icing sugar, sieved

1 Put the butter and milk into a small saucepan and heat gently to melt. When melted, pour into the mixer bowl with the flour, yeast, sugar, eggs and salt. With the dough hook, mix on speed 4 for 3 minutes until combined. Cover and leave in a warm, draught-free place for 30 minutes.

2 Preheat the oven to 160°C/Gas Mark 3. Remove the dough from the mixer bowl and divide into 24 equal-sized pieces. Roll each piece into a sausage shape and roll them in the icing sugar.

3 Lay three pieces of dough side by side and press the ends of these together. Plait the three pieces, pressing the other ends together to finish. Repeat with the remaining dough to make eight rolls. Transfer to a baking sheet and leave to stand for 30 minutes. Cook the rolls in the oven for 20 minutes until golden brown, and serve warm.

LEMON BRIOCHE
A cake-like French bread made with eggs and butter and flavoured here with lemon. It puffs up to form a loaf that is perfect for a light breakfast, served warm with butter and jam.

MAKES ONE 500-g LOAF

Preparation time: 25 minutes plus 2 hours
10 minutes rising time

Cooking time: 30 minutes

Attachments used

2 Tbsp caster sugar

3 Tbsp water

1 packet (7 g) active dry yeast

2 eggs

200 g plain flour

$^1/_4$ tsp salt

Grated rind of 1 lemon

90 g unsalted butter, cubed

1 egg yolk, to glaze

1 Tbsp water, to glaze

1 Put 1 tablespoon of sugar in a small saucepan with the water and dissolve the sugar over a low heat. Sprinkle the yeast onto the mixture and leave to stand for 5 to 10 minutes until frothy. Stir the yeast into the liquid and beat in the eggs.

2 Put the flour, salt, lemon rind and remaining sugar into the mixer bowl and, with the dough hook, blend the ingredients on speed 1.

3 Increasing to speed 3, gradually add the yeast mixture to form a dough and then knead for a further 2 to 3 minutes, scraping the dough down the sides of the bowl as required. Add the butter to the mixture, mixing on speed 6 for 3 minutes until fully combined.

4 Put the dough in a large oiled bowl, cover with a clean, damp tea towel and leave to rise in a warm, draught-free place for 1 hour 30 minutes until doubled in bulk.

5 Grease a 500-g tin with butter. Knead the dough two or three times on a lightly floured board and divide into eight even-sized pieces. Roll each piece into a ball and place in the tin. Cover and leave to prove for 40 minutes.

6 Preheat the oven to 200°C/Gas Mark 6. Mix the egg yolk and water to form a glaze and brush over the top of the dough. Cook in the oven for 30 minutes until the loaf is golden brown. Unmould the loaf immediately and serve warm with butter and jam.

CROISSANTS
If the butter oozes out of this rich, French pastry dough while you are rolling and folding, slide the dough onto a baking sheet and chill until it is easier to handle.

MAKES 12

Preparation time: 30 minutes plus 1 hour chilling and 2 hours rising time

Cooking time: 15 minutes

Attachments used

350 g plain flour
1/2 tsp salt
1 Tbsp caster sugar
1 packet (7 g) active dry yeast
75 ml/1/3 cup near-boiling water
75 ml/1/3 cup milk
175 g unsalted butter
1 egg, beaten

1 Sieve the flour and salt into the mixer bowl. Add the sugar and yeast and mix together for a few seconds with the dough hook on speed 1.

2 Mix the water and milk and check the temperature with your finger – it should be tepid. Still on speed 1, pour the liquid into a well in the flour and mix together. Then knead the dough on speed 2 for 2 minutes until smooth and elastic. Cover with clingfilm and leave in a warm place to rise for about an hour, or until doubled in size

3 Punch down the dough and turn out onto a floured surface. Knead until smooth. Wrap in a tea towel and refrigerate for 10 minutes.

4 Put the butter between two sheets of clingfilm and roll into a rectangle. Fold the butter in half and roll out again. Repeat until it is pliable, but still cold, then flatten to form it into a 15 x 10-cm rectangle.

5 On a floured surface, roll out the dough to a rectangle, about 30 x 15 cm. With one short side facing you, place the block of butter in the centre. Fold the bottom third of the dough over the butter and then fold the top third down over the two. Press the open sides together to seal.

6 Half-turn the dough, clockwise. Roll out to a rectangle and repeat the folding process twice more, then wrap and chill for 30 minutes. Repeat the rolling and folding process twice more. Chill for a final 30 minutes.

7 Dampen two baking sheets with water. Roll the chilled dough to a rectangle, about 45 x 30 cm. Cut into six even-sized squares, then cut each square in half diagonally.

8 Starting at the base of each triangle, roll up loosely, and secure the point with a little beaten egg. Arrange point-side down on the baking sheets, curving the ends to form a crescent shape. Lightly brush with the beaten egg, then cover with oiled clingfilm and leave to prove in a warm draught-free place for about one hour, or until doubled in size.

9 Preheat the oven to 220°C/Gas Mark 8. Remove the clingfilm and brush again with the egg glaze. Bake for 3 minutes, then lower the temperature to 190°C/Gas Mark 5 and bake for a further 10 to 12 minutes, until golden and crisp. Leave on the baking sheets for a few minutes, then transfer to a wire rack. Serve warm or cold.

VARIATIONS

ALMOND CROISSANTS – Using the flat beater, on speed 4, blend 40 g butter and 100 g caster sugar together. Beat in 1 egg yolk and 100 g ground almonds to make a thick paste. Place a tablespoonful of the paste about 2 cm up from the base of each triangle before rolling up the croissants. Scatter a few flaked almonds over the top before baking and serve lightly dusted with icing sugar.

CHOCOLATE CROISSANTS – Using the rotary slicer/shredder with the coarse shredding drum attached, on speed 4, grate 75 g plain, milk or white chocolate and divide among the triangles of croissant dough, about 2 cm up from the base, then roll up as before.

DESSERTS AND DRINKS

PASTRIES
The KitchenAid mixer makes wonderful pastry because it does not overhandle the dough, keeping it cool and easy to work with. These four basic pastries can be used to make simple tarts or more elaborate desserts.

STRUDEL PASTRY
This is one pastry that doesn't need gentle handling – the more stretching and beating the better to develop the gluten in the flour. It isn't difficult to make, but you do need a large work surface to roll it out until almost transparent.

MAKES ABOUT 275 g (enough for 1 large strudel)

Preparation time: 40 minutes plus 30 minutes resting time

225 g strong white bread flour
1/2 tsp salt
1 egg, beaten
2 tsp sunflower oil
About 150 ml/2/3 cup warm water

Attachments used

1 Sieve the flour and salt into the mixer bowl and mix with the dough hook on speed 1. Stir the egg and oil into the water and with the machine still running, slowly add to the flour and mix to a soft, sticky dough.

2 Knead with the dough hook on speed 2 for 4 to 5 minutes until the dough is smooth and elastic. Cover the bowl with a tea towel or clingfilm and leave the dough to rest for 30 minutes.

3 Lightly flour a very large clean cloth, such as a tablecloth. Roll out the dough very thinly, lifting it frequently to prevent it sticking. Gently roll and stretch the dough with your hands until it forms a 60 cm square. Use a pair of sharp scissors to trim off the thick edges. Use straight away.

FLAKY PASTRY
Light, crisp and buttery, flaky pastry is similar to puff pastry, but simpler. Instead of adding the fat in one piece, it is incorporated by dotting it over the rolled-out dough, creating pockets of air that help separate the many layers.

MAKES ABOUT 450 g

Preparation time: 20 minutes plus 2 hours chilling time

225 g plain or strong white bread flour
Pinch of salt
170 g chilled butter, or half butter and half white vegetable fat or lard
150 ml/2/3 cup chilled water

Attachments used

1 Sieve the flour and salt into the mixer bowl. Cut 50 g of the butter into cubes and scatter over the flour mixture, then using the flat beater on speed 2, blend until the mixture resembles breadcrumbs.

2 Using the flat beater on speed 1, gradually pour the water into the bowl and mix to form a soft dough. Wrap in clingfilm and chill for 30 minutes.

3 On a lightly floured surface, roll out the dough to a rectangle about 30 x 10 cm. Cut 40 g of the remaining butter into tiny pieces and dot them evenly all over the top two-thirds of the pastry, leaving a good margin around the edges.

4 Fold the bottom third of the pastry up and over the butter and then fold the top third of the dough down over the two. Press the open sides of the parcel together with the rolling pin to seal in the butter. Wrap in clingfilm and chill for 10 minutes.

5 Give the dough a half turn, clockwise. Repeat the rolling and folding process, this time without adding any butter, then wrap and chill for 10 minutes. Roll out two more times, using 40 g butter each time. Wrap and chill again for 10 minutes. Roll out and fold again, without adding any butter. Wrap and chill for at least one hour, before using.

CHOUX PASTRY
Choux pastry puffs up to more than double its original size during baking to make a hollow centre, which is perfect for stuffing with a sweet or savoury filling.

MAKES ABOUT 150 g
(enough for 20 small puffs or 12 éclairs)
Preparation time: 10 minutes

Attachments used

65 g plain flour
Pinch of salt
50 g butter
150 ml/^{2}/$_3$ cup water
2 eggs, beaten

1 Sieve the flour and salt into a bowl or onto a sheet of greaseproof paper. Gently heat the butter and water in a saucepan until melted.

2 Increase the heat and as soon as the liquid is boiling fast, tip in all the flour and beat vigorously to form a smooth paste. Beat the mixture over a low heat until it begins to form a ball and leave the sides of the pan; this will take about 30 seconds.

3 Remove the pan from the heat and tip the mixture into the mixer bowl. Leave to cool for a minute or two.

4 Gradually add the eggs, beating well between each addition with the flat beater on speed 4, until you have a shiny paste. You may not need all the egg. The mixture is ready when it falls reluctantly from a spoon.

PÂTE SABLÉE
A rich, crisp-textured sweet pastry used mainly for tartlet and flan cases because it holds its shape well. The high proportion of sugar makes it softer than basic shortcrust pastry, so it needs to be well chilled before rolling and baking.

MAKES ABOUT 275 g
(enough for a 23-cm flan tin or eight 7-cm tartlet tins)
Preparation time: 10 minutes plus 1 hour chilling time

Attachments used

150 g plain flour
Pinch of salt
75 g chilled butter
25 g icing sugar
2 egg yolks
1 tsp chilled water
^{1}/$_2$ tsp vanilla essence (optional)

1 Sieve the flour and salt into the mixer bowl. Cut the butter into cubes and scatter over the flour mixture, then using the flat beater on speed 2, blend until the mixture resembles breadcrumbs.

2 Lift the beater and sieve the icing sugar over the rubbed-in mixture. Whisk together the egg yolks, water and vanilla essence, if using, in a small bowl and sprinkle over the mixture.

3 Using the flat beater, blend for just a few seconds on speed 1 until the pastry begins to hold together. Test the dough by pinching a piece between your fingers; if it is still too crumbly add another teaspoon of chilled water and mix again.

4 Gather the dough together to form a ball, then knead on a lightly floured surface with just the heel of your hand for about a minute.

5 Shape the pastry back into a ball, then flatten into a flat round (this makes it easier when you start to roll it out). Wrap in clingfilm and chill in the refrigerator for about an hour before using. If you store it in the refrigerator for longer, leave out at room temperature for about 10 minutes before rolling out.

PASTRY CREAMS All these pastry creams can be used to fill pastries, cakes, tarts or choux buns.

The crème anglaise is a rich custard to pour over desserts. All can be flavoured with vanilla, almond or even chocolate.

CRÈME PÂTISSIÈRE (Confectioner's custard) This pastry cream is the classic filling for fruit-topped flans and tarts and can

be piped into choux pastry buns. It's best made the day before so that it can be well-chilled before use.

MAKES ABOUT 350 ml/1^1/$_2$ CUPS

(enough for a 20-cm pastry case)

Preparation time: 10 minutes plus 10 minutes infusing time

Cooking time: 5 minutes

300 ml/1^1/$_4$ cups milk

1 vanilla pod, split, or ^{1}/$_2$ tsp vanilla essence

3 egg yolks

50 g caster sugar

2 Tbsp plain flour

2 Tbsp cornflour

Attachments used

1 Pour the milk into a heavy-based saucepan, add the vanilla pod if using, and slowly bring to the boil. Take off the heat and leave to infuse for 10 minutes. Remove the vanilla pod.

2 Put the egg yolks and sugar in the mixer bowl and beat with the wire whip on speed 4 for 2 minutes or until very pale and thick. Gradually sieve the flour and cornflour over the creamed mixture and beat until blended.

3 Bring the milk back to the boil and slowly pour over the creamed mixture, mixing with the wire whip on speed 1.

4 Pour the crème pâtissière into the saucepan and cook over a low heat, stirring with a wooden spoon until the mixture comes to the boil and thickens. Gently simmer for a minute, stirring all the time. Remove from the heat and stir in the vanilla essence, if using instead of the vanilla pod.

5 Transfer the crème pâtissière to a bowl and cover the surface with cling film or a piece of damp baking parchment to prevent a skin forming as it cools.

CRÈME MOUSSELINE Crème mousseline is made by beating butter into crème pâtissière to give it a light, fluffy texture.

It is a delicious alternative to cream in éclairs and puff pastries as it retains its texture and won't soak into the pastry.

MAKES ABOUT 500 ml/2^1/$_4$ CUPS

Preparation time: 10 minutes

50 g caster sugar

100 g unsalted butter, at room temperature

350 ml/1^1/$_2$ cups warm crème pâtissière (page 120)

Attachments used

1 Add the caster sugar and 25 g of the butter to the warm crème pâtissière and stir until blended. Cover the surface with clingfilm and leave to cool.

2 Put the remaining butter in the mixer bowl and beat with the ffat beater on speed 4 for 2 minutes, or until pale.

3 On speed 1, beat in the cold crème pâtissière a tablespoon at a time with the flat beater, until the mixture is pale and fluffy. Use straight away, or cover and store in the refrigerator, then leave out at room temperature for 5 minutes before using.

CRÈME DESSERT
A sweet, thick cream made by adding egg yolks and caster sugar to crème fraîche, a cultured cream.

Serve a spoonful with a cake, fruit flan or hot baked fruit.

MAKES ABOUT 350 g
Preparation time: 5 minutes

Attachments used

4 egg yolks
150 g caster sugar
100 ml/¹/₂ cup crème fraîche

1 Put the egg yolks and sugar in the mixer bowl and beat with the wire whip on speed 4 for 2 minutes, or until very pale and thick.

2 On speed 1, add the crème fraîche a tablespoon at a time, until just mixed, taking care not to overbeat or the crème dessert will lose its fluffy texture.

VARIATIONS

VANILLA CRÈME DESSERT – Add 1 teaspoon of vanilla essence with the crème fraîche.

CARAMEL CRÈME DESSERT – Use soft light brown sugar instead of caster sugar.

CRÈME ANGLAISE
This thin egg custard can be served hot or chilled. Here it's made with the addition of a little cornflour to reduce the risk of curdling, but you can leave it out if you prefer.

MAKES ABOUT 350 ml/1¹/₂ CUPS
Preparation time: 10 minutes plus 10 minutes infusing time
Cooking time: 5 minutes

Attachments used

300 ml/1¹/₄ cups milk, or a mixture of milk and single or double cream
1 vanilla pod, split, or ¹/₂ tsp vanilla essence
3 egg yolks
1 Tbsp caster sugar
1 tsp cornflour

1 Pour the milk into a heavy-based saucepan, add the vanilla pod if using and bring slowly to the boil. Take off the heat, then leave to infuse for 10 minutes. Remove the vanilla pod.

2 Put the egg yolks, caster sugar and cornflour in the mixer bowl. Beat with the wire whip on speed 2 until pale and thick.

3 Bring the milk back to the boil, then using the wire whip on speed 1, slowly pour into the egg and sugar mixture and mix together.

4 Pour the mixture back into the saucepan, then cook over a low heat, stirring constantly until the custard thickens enough to lightly coat the back of a wooden spoon. Stir in the vanilla essence, if using.

5 Serve hot or cold. If serving cold, pour into a chilled bowl and cover the surface with clingfilm or a piece of damp baking parchment to prevent a skin forming. Cool, then chill until ready to serve.

VARIATIONS

CITRUS CRÈME ANGLAISE – Infuse the milk with a finely pared strip of orange, lemon or lime rind instead of vanilla.

CHOCOLATE CRÈME ANGLAISE – Melt 50 g chopped plain chocolate with the milk.

CRÊPES (Pancakes) Thin, wispy French pancakes that can be eaten on their own with just a squeeze of lemon and sugar or filled with chicken, vegetables or cheese, or something sweet, as here.

MAKES 10

Preparation time: 10 minutes

Cooking time: 35 minutes

Attachments used

125 g plain flour

40 g caster sugar

2 eggs

1 egg yolk

100 ml/^{1}/$_2$ cup double cream

100 ml/^{1}/$_2$ cup milk

50 g butter

300 g eating apples, peeled, cored and diced

150 g raisins

Grated rind and juice of 1 lemon

3 Tbsp Calvados

Butter, for frying

Caster sugar, for dredging

1 Sieve the flour into the mixer bowl and add the sugar. With the wire whip on speed 1, gradually add the eggs, egg yolk, cream and milk to make a batter. Mix for a further 1 minute on speed 4 to remove any lumps. Leave the batter to stand.

2 Meanwhile, put the butter into a saucepan with the diced apple, raisins, lemon juice and rind and the Calvados. Cook over a medium heat for 5 to 7 minutes until the apples have softened.

3 Melt a little butter in a crêpe pan and pour off any excess. Spoon a tenth of the batter into the pan, swirling to coat the base with batter. Cook for 2 minutes until the underside is browned, flip the crêpe over and cook for a further minute. Remove from the pan and keep the crêpe warm while cooking the remaining batter to make ten crêpes.

4 Spoon the apple filling into the centre of each crêpe, roll the crêpes up and sprinkle with caster sugar. Serve warm.

BELGIAN WAFFLES
Waffles are made in a special waffle iron, which gives them their honeycombed appearance. Serve with maple syrup, ice cream or icing sugar and strawberries. They can also be eaten with bacon and maple syrup for breakfast.

MAKES 8

Preparation time: 15 minutes plus 1 hour standing time

Cooking time: 25 minutes

Attachments used

300 ml/1¼ cups milk

200 ml/ ¾ cup double cream

250 g plain flour

70 g caster sugar

1 tsp active dry yeast

4 eggs, separated

150 g butter, melted and cooled

Pinch of salt

Maple syrup, to serve (optional)

1 Warm the milk and cream to just below boiling point and set aside. Put the flour, 50 g of the sugar and the yeast in the mixer bowl. Using the flat beater, mix on speed 1 for 30 seconds. Stir in the egg yolks and mix on speed 2 for 2 minutes.

2 Add the milk and cream and the melted butter. Change to the wire whip and mix on speed 6 until a thick, smooth batter is formed. Transfer to a large bowl, cover and leave to stand at room temperature for 1 hour.

3 Clean the mixer bowl and the wire whip and dry thoroughly, then whisk the egg whites with a pinch of salt on speed 8 for 30 seconds until the egg whites are stiff. Add the remaining sugar and whisk again until peaking.

4 Fold the egg whites into the batter with a metal spoon and heat the waffle iron according to manufacturer's instructions. Pour enough batter into the iron to coat the base thinly, close the iron and cook for 2 to 3 minutes, turning the iron if it is not an electric model. The waffle is cooked when golden brown and crisp and it can be easily removed from the iron. Continue with the remaining batter and serve the waffles hot, with maple syrup.

KAISERSCHMARREN (Emperor pancakes) A fluffy pancake named after an Austrian Emperor and sprinkled with fried

raisins, a little sugar and cinnamon just before serving.

SERVES 8

Preparation time: 10 minutes

Cooking time: 8 minutes

Attachments used

4 eggs

85 g butter

60 g caster sugar

Pinch of salt

100 g plain flour

150 ml/^{2}/$_3$ cup milk

75 g raisins

Oil, for frying

1 Tbsp caster sugar, to sprinkle

^{1}/$_2$ tsp ground cinnamon, to sprinkle

1   Separate the eggs and put the whites into the mixer bowl. With the wire whip, whisk the egg whites for 1 minute on speed 8 until stiff and peaking. Remove from the mixer bowl and reserve.

2   Change to the flat beater, and put 60 g of the butter, the sugar and egg yolks into the bowl and blend these together, beginning on speed 4 and increasing to speed 6, for 1 minute. Blend in the salt, flour and milk on speed 4 for 1 minute, then carefully mix in the egg whites.

3   Heat the remaining butter in a small pan and fry the raisins over a medium heat for 1 minute. Remove and set aside. Heat the oil in a large frying pan, add the egg mixture and cook over a medium heat for 4 to 5 minutes until cooked underneath and the centre is set. Carefully flip the mixture over and cook for a further 3 to 4 minutes until cooked through.

4   Using two forks, cut the mixture into wedges and transfer to a warm serving plate. Sprinkle the raisins over the top with the sugar and ground cinnamon. Serve hot.

For recipes that require butter or margarine, you will need to use the flat beater rather than the wire whip to blend the ingredients, as fats can get stuck in the whip. It is very easy and quick to change the attachments, even in the middle of the recipe.

DAMPFKNÖDEL

(Sweet steamed dumplings) These German dumplings are cooked in a hot mixture of sugar, butter and water so that the hot top and bottom brown, while the middle stays white and soft. They are eaten here with a custard sauce.

SERVES 6

Preparation time: 20 minutes plus 50 minutes rising time

Cooking time: 50 minutes

Attachments used

250 ml/1 cup milk

1 packet (7 g) active dry yeast

50 g caster sugar

2 large eggs

2 Tbsp vegetable oil

1 tsp salt

Grated rind of 1 lemon

500 g strong white bread flour

2 Tbsp butter

For the custard sauce

2 eggs

1 Tbsp caster sugar

250 ml/1 cup milk

1/2 tsp vanilla essence

For cooking the dumplings

6 Tbsp butter

6 Tbsp caster sugar

250 ml/1 cup water

1 Warm the milk in a pan to lukewarm. Stir in the yeast and 1 teaspoon sugar, mixing until dissolved. Put the mixture in the mixer bowl and add the rest of the sugar, the eggs, oil, salt, lemon rind, 350 g flour, and 2 tablespoons butter. With the dough hook, mix on speed 2 for 1 minute until a smooth, soft dough forms. Add any extra flour as required.

2 Knead the dough with the dough hook on speed 1 for 5 minutes until smooth. Transfer the dough to a lightly oiled bowl, cover and leave to prove in a warm, draught-free place for 30 minutes until doubled in bulk.

3 Meanwhile, make the custard sauce by putting the eggs, sugar and 3 tablespoons milk in the mixer bowl. Bring the remaining milk to the boil in a saucepan with the vanilla essence. Pour the milk on to the eggs and mix on speed 1 for 30 seconds using the flat beater. Transfer the

mixture to the saucepan and cook over a gentle heat until the mixture coats the back of a wooden spoon. Do not boil.

4 Shape the dough into 12 even-sized balls and put on a baking sheet lined with greaseproof paper. Cover and leave to prove for 15 to 20 minutes.

5 To cook the dumplings, put 2 tablespoons butter in a saucepan with 2 tablespoons sugar and a third of the water. Cover and bring to the boil. Add four dumplings at a time to the pan and cover. Reduce the heat and cook for 15 to 20 minutes. The dumplings fry when they are cooked and the water has evaporated. Remove them from the pan, keep warm and repeat until all the dumplings are cooked, adding the same quantity of butter, sugar and water to the pan for each batch. Serve with the custard sauce, and decorate with grated lemon rind.

ŒUFS À LA NEIGE (Eggs in snow)

A light, French dessert of meringues floating in a crème anglaise sauce. You can buy vanilla sugar, or make your own by keeping a vanilla pod in a jar of caster sugar for at least two weeks before using.

SERVES 6

Preparation time: 20 minutes

Cooking time: 15 minutes plus 30 minutes chilling

Attachments used

3 eggs, separated

Pinch of salt

150 g vanilla sugar

450 ml/2 cups milk

150 ml/²/₃ cup single cream

1 Tbsp orange flower water (optional)

For the caramel

175 g caster sugar

3 Tbsp cold water

1 Using the wire whip on speed 6, beat the egg whites until frothy. Add the salt and beat on speed 8 until soft peaks form. Gradually add 125 g of the vanilla sugar, a tablespoon at a time, beating well after each addition until the mixture is very stiff and shiny.

2 Pour the milk and cream into a wide saucepan and bring to a gentle simmer. Using two spoons, shape five or six ovals of meringue, carefully dropping them into the pan as you make them. Poach for 2 to 3 minutes, or until they have doubled in size and are firm.

3 Remove the meringues with a slotted spoon and drain on kitchen paper. Repeat with the remaining mixture - you should have about 18 meringues, depending on their size.

4 Put the egg yolks and the remaining vanilla sugar into the mixer bowl and beat with the wire whip on speed 4 until pale and creamy. Bring the milk and cream back to the boil, and with the wire whip on speed 1, slowly pour over the egg yolks.

5 Pour the mixture back into the pan and heat gently, stirring all the time, until the custard thickens slightly and coats the back of a wooden spoon, taking care not to boil it or it may curdle. Stir in the orange flower water, if using. Pour the custard into a serving dish and arrange the meringues on top. Cool, then chill for 30 minutes.

6 To make the caramel, put the sugar in a heavy-based saucepan with the water and heat gently until it is completely dissolved. Increase the heat and boil rapidly for a few minutes until a rich golden brown colour, gently swirling the pan to ensure even browning.

7 Carefully drizzle the caramel onto an oiled baking sheet in zigzag patterns. Leave to cool and harden, then lift the caramel off and use to decorate the meringues and custard. Serve straight away.

CHOCOLATE MOUSSE

A classic rich French dessert, made even lighter by whisking the dark chocolate, cream and eggs with the wire whip. Serve with a coulis or a crème anglaise and chocolate shavings.

SERVES 4

Preparation time: 15 minutes plus chilling time

Attachments used

225 g bitter dark chocolate

1 Tbsp brandy or water

4 eggs, separated

3 Tbsp double cream

1 Break the chocolate into squares and melt with the brandy or water in a double boiler or in a heatproof bowl over, but not touching, a saucepan of boiling water.

2 Put the melted chocolate and egg yolks in the mixer bowl and, with the wire whip, beat on speed 2 until thick and creamy.

3 Changing to speed 1 and still using the wire whip, add the cream until fully incorporated. Transfer the mixture to a large bowl.

4 Clean the mixer bowl and the wire whip and dry thoroughly, then whisk the egg whites with the wire whip on speed 8, until stiff and peaking. Fold into the chocolate mixture until well combined.

5 Spoon the mixture into serving dishes and chill for at least 1 hour before serving.

GERMKNÖDEL

(Plum dumplings) A sweet Austrian dumpling enclosing a spoonful of plum jam and served with a sauce of vanilla butter. You can substitute any fruit jam you like for the plum jam.

MAKES 8

Preparation time: 20 minutes plus 1 hour 30 minutes standing time

Cooking time: 40 minutes

Attachments used

500 g plain flour

1 packet (7 g) active dry yeast

250 ml/1 cup warm milk

30 g caster sugar

2 eggs

30 g butter, melted

1 tsp salt

3 drops lemon essence

8 tsp plum jam

1 Tbsp vanilla sugar

2 Tbsp butter

1 Sieve the flour into the mixer bowl and make a well in the centre. Add the yeast, 5 tablespoons milk, the sugar, eggs, melted butter, salt and lemon essence. With the dough hook, mix on speed 2 for 30 seconds, increasing to speed 4. Still using the dough hook on speed 2, gradually add as much of the remaining milk as required to make a non-sticky dough. Cover the bowl and leave to stand in a warm, draught-free place for 45 minutes to 1 hour, until doubled in bulk.

2 Knead the dough for 1 to 2 minutes on speed 4, then separate into eight equal-sized pieces and shape into dumplings the size of a snowball. Make a thumb imprint in the centre of each dumpling and spoon a teaspoon of plum jam into each. Reshape the dumplings around the jam to encase completely. Put onto a baking sheet lined with greaseproof paper and leave in a warm, draught-free place for a further 30 minutes.

3 Bring a large saucepan of water to the boil and add four of the dumplings. Cover and boil for 20 minutes until cooked through. Remove with a draining spoon and keep warm while cooking the remaining dumplings.

4 Meanwhile, heat the vanilla sugar and butter in a small saucepan until melted. Put the dumplings onto a warm plate and pour the butter and sugar mixture over just before serving.

TARTE AU CITRON
An exquisite lemon tart, which should be both sharp and sweet like the lemons it is made from. A sweet pastry is used here, though you could also use a plain rich shortcrust.

The best way to squeeze the juice out of your lemons is to use one hand to stabilize the KitchenAid mixer while juicing the fruit with your other hand. You can set the mixer bowl at a lower level to catch the juice, or place a glass or jug directly underneath the juicer.

SERVES 6 TO 8

Preparation time: 15 minutes plus 2 hours chilling time

Cooking time: 35 minutes

Attachments used

1 quantity pâte sablée (page 119)

5 lemons, preferably unwaxed

5 medium eggs

1/4 tsp salt

250 g caster sugar

150 g butter

Icing sugar, to dust

1 Preheat the oven to 200°C/Gas Mark 6. Roll the pastry out into a circle on a lightly floured surface and use to line a greased 24-cm loose-bottomed flan tin. Make a few holes in the pastry with a fork, fill with some dried beans and blind bake for 10 minutes. Take out the beans and bake in the oven for a further 15 minutes. Remove the pastry case from the oven and take out of the tin. Set aside to cool.

2 Grate the rind from the lemons and reserve, then cut the lemons in half. Using the citrus juicer, on speed 6, squeeze out the juice and pour into a saucepan.

3 Bring the lemon juice to the boil. Meanwhile, place the eggs with the salt, sugar and reserved lemon rind in the mixer bowl. Fit the wire whip and whisk well on speed 4. Still using the wire whip, gradually pour in the hot lemon juice while whisking. When all the lemon juice has been added, return to the cleaned saucepan and cook over a low heat, stirring continuously until the mixture thickens and coats the back of a wooden spoon.

4 Return the mixture to the cleaned mixer bowl and with the flat beater, on speed 6, gradually beat in the butter a little at a time. Pour the mixture into the pastry case and chill in the refrigerator for at least 2 hours before serving. Serve dusted with icing sugar.

TARTE AU CHOCOLAT ET À LA FRAMBOISE Raspberries and chocolate

combine with a light lemon pastry in this classic French dessert – try replacing the raspberries with thin slices of mango or banana.

SERVES 6

Preparation time: 20 minutes plus 3 hours standing

Cooking time: About 30 minutes

Attachments used

For the lemon pastry

200 g plain flour

50 g icing sugar

Grated zest of 1/4 lemon

150 g butter

3 Tbsp ground almonds

1 egg

Large pinch of salt

For the filling

300 g dark cooking chocolate

2 Tbsp crème fraîche

100 g butter

350 g raspberries, cut in halves

1   Preheat the oven to 210°C/Gas Mark 6. Place the flour, icing sugar, lemon zest, butter, ground almonds, egg and salt into the mixer bowl and, using the dough hook, mix on speed 1 to 2 until the pastry leaves the sides of the bowl clean. Shape into a ball, press down and repeat two more times. Wrap in clingfilm and leave to rest in a cool place for 3 hours.

2   To make the topping, melt the chocolate in a double boiler or in a heat proof bowl over, but not touching, a saucepan of boiling water. Place the crème fraîche in a small saucepan and bring almost to boiling, then pour into the melted chocolate. Cut the butter into small knobs and mix in.

3   Roll the pastry out into a circle on a lightly floured surface and use to line a greased tart tin. Make a few holes in the pastry with a fork, fill with some dried beans and blind bake for 10 minutes. Take out the beans and bake in the oven for a further 15 minutes. Remove the pastry case from the oven and take out of the tin. Set aside to cool.

4   Arrange the raspberries in the bottom of the pastry case and cover with the chocolate mixture. Set aside for 30 minutes to cool, and then chill in the refrigerator for 1 1/2 hours until the chocolate has set sufficiently to enable easy slicing.

POTS DE CRÈME AU CHOCOLAT Delicious little chocolate custards, made with just cream and

egg yolks, that are indulgently rich. Ramekins or martini glasses would also make stunning petits pots.

SERVES 6

Preparation time: 30 minutes plus 2 hours chilling time

Cooking time: 20 minutes

Attachments used

450 ml/2 cups double cream

1 Tbsp sugar

4 squares (25 g each) chocolate, melted

3 egg yolks

1 Preheat the oven to 170°C/Gas Mark 3. Heat the cream and the sugar in a double boiler or in a heatproof bowl over, but not touching, a saucepan of boiling water, stirring until the sugar has dissolved. Add the chocolate, stirring until well blended. Remove from the heat and set aside.

2 Place the egg yolks in the mixer bowl. Using the wire whip, on speed 8, whisk for 1 minute. Reduce to speed 2 and gradually add the cream mixture, whipping until well blended.

3 Fill six 150-ml/2/3-cup custard cups or crème pots two-thirds full. Place the cups in a roasting tin and add enough boiling water to come halfway up the sides of the cups. Bake in the oven for 18 to 20 minutes or until firm. Chill for at least 2 hours before serving.

RAISIN CHEESECAKE
This German version of the classic baked cheesecake is made with quark, a fresh curd cheese that can be lower in fat than the cream cheese often used to make cheesecakes..

SERVES 10 TO 12

Preparation time: 15 minutes plus 30 minutes chilling time and cooling time

Cooking time: 1 hour 15 minutes

For the base

225 g plain flour

100 g butter, softened

100 g caster sugar

1 egg

Pinch of salt

1 tsp baking powder

For the filling

750 g quark

250 ml/1 cup sour cream

225 g caster sugar

4 eggs

Grated rind of half a lemon

1/4 tsp vanilla essence

125 g raisins

60 g cornflour

1 tsp plain flour

1 tsp baking powder

75 g slivered almonds

Attachments used

1 To make the base, sieve the flour into the mixer bowl. Add the butter, sugar, egg, salt and baking powder, then, with the flat beater, mix on speed 2 for 2 minutes, until a smooth dough forms. Remove the dough from the bowl and wrap in a plastic bag. Chill for 30 minutes.

2 Preheat the oven to 190°C/Gas Mark 5. Place all of the filling ingredients, except the almonds, in the mixer bowl and mix with the flat beater on speed 2 for 1 minute, until thoroughly combined.

3 Remove the dough from the refrigerator, roll out on a heavily floured surface and use to line the base and sides of a 20-cm springform tin. Cook in the oven for 15 minutes.

4 Pour the filling into the partly cooked base and sprinkle the almonds over the top. Cook in the oven for 1 hour until cooked through. Turn the oven off and leave the cheesecake in the oven to cool. Serve chilled.

SCHWARZWÄLDEKIRSCHTORTE This is a modern approach to the famous Black Forest Gateau. Use

fresh cherries if they are available, or canned, sour Morello cherries, making sure they are first thoroughly drained.

SERVES 8

Preparation time: 25 minutes plus overnight standing

Cooking time: 25 minutes

Attachments used

175 g plain dark chocolate

6 Tbsp kirsch or brandy

225 g caster sugar

5 medium eggs, separated

300 ml/1¼ cups double cream

2–3 Tbsp icing sugar

350 g fresh cherries, stoned, or 400-g can Morello cherries, drained

Extra cherries, to decorate

1 Preheat the oven to 180ºC/Gas Mark 4. Lightly oil and line a Swiss roll tin with greaseproof paper, ensuring that the paper stands about 5 cm above the sides of the tin.

2 Break the chocolate into small pieces and place in a double boiler or in a heatproof bowl over, but not touching, a saucepan of boiling water. Add 4 tablespoons of the kirsch or brandy and heat gently until the chocolate has melted. Stir until smooth, then remove from the heat.

3 Place the caster sugar with the egg yolks in the mixer bowl and, using the wire whip on speed 8, beat until the mixture is very thick and creamy, then add the melted chocolate and beat again until thoroughly incorporated. Spoon into another bowl.

4 Clean the mixer bowl and the wire whip and dry thoroughly, then whisk the egg whites on speed 10, until very stiff. Fold 1 tablespoon of the egg white into the chocolate mixture and then carefully stir in the remaining egg white with a spoon. Stir lightly together, taking care not to over-mix, then turn into the prepared tin. Tap lightly on the surface to level it and to remove any air bubbles.

5 Bake in the oven for 20 to 25 minutes or until the top is set. Remove from the oven and cover with a damp sheet of greaseproof paper and a clean tea towel. Leave overnight or for at least 8 hours.

6 When ready to serve, whip the cream in the mixer bowl, using the wire whip on speed 8, and stir in the remaining kirsch or brandy. Sprinkle a large sheet of greaseproof paper with the icing sugar and invert the cooked cake onto the icing sugar paper. Remove the tin and discard the lining paper.

7 Spread with the whipped cream and top with the cherries, carefully roll up and place on a serving plate. If you like, sprinkle with extra icing sugar and decorate with the extra cherries.

KOLDSKAAL
A Danish cream pudding made with buttermilk and vanilla that can be poured over any soft fruit in season or just eaten with a spoonful of fruit jam. Serve with the kammerjunker biscuits below.

MAKES 1.2 LITRES/5 CUPS

Preparation time: 10 minutes

Attachments used

4 egg yolks

$1/2$ tsp vanilla essence

100 g caster sugar

Juice of half a small lemon

1 litre/4 cups buttermilk

Quartered strawberries and sliced bananas, to serve

1 Put the egg yolks, vanilla essence and sugar in the mixer bowl and, with the wire whip, whisk the ingredients together on speed 4, increasing to speed 6, for 2 to 3 minutes until frothy.

2 Still using the wire whip on speed 6, very slowly add the lemon juice until the mixture is very frothy. Increase to speed 8 and whisk for 1 minute. Return to speed 6 and gradually pour in the buttermilk until fully incorporated.

3 Divide the fruit among the serving dishes and spoon the koldskaal over the top. Serve with kammerjunker.

KAMMERJUNKER
Hard, little Danish biscuits, which are baked twice and can be served with a cream dessert like the koldskaal above, ice cream or a cup of coffee. This recipe makes 70 tiny biscuits, which can be stored in an airtight container.

MAKES 70 SMALL RUSKS

Preparation time: 10 minutes

Cooking time: 35 minutes

Attachments used

325 g plain flour

125 g butter, diced

100 g caster sugar

1 tsp baking powder

Grated rind of 1 lemon

1 egg

100 ml/$1/2$ cup milk

1 Preheat the oven to 220°C/Gas Mark 7. Sieve the flour into the mixer bowl, add the butter and, using the flat beater on speed 1, mix in until fully incorporated.

2 Add the sugar, baking powder and lemon rind and mix for a further 30 seconds. Lightly whisk the egg and milk together and blend into the mixture using the flat beater on speed 1. Continue to mix for 1 minute to knead the dough.

3 Turn out onto a floured surface and roll into thin 35-cm long sausages. Cut the dough into walnut sized balls and transfer to a non-stick baking sheet. Cook in the preheated oven for 8 to 10 minutes until golden brown.

4 Remove the tray from the oven and cut the biscuits in half. Return them to the oven, turn the oven off and leave them to crisp in the remaining heat for 25 minutes. Serve with the koldskaal.

GALETTES À LA FRANGIPANE (Almond pastries) Little round, flat cakes made here from flaky pastry and

filled with a liqueur-soaked almond crème pâtissière. You could use ready-made pastry instead of making your own.

SERVES 4

Preparation time: 45 minutes plus 30 minutes chilling time

Cooking time: 20 minutes

Attachments used

50 g softened unsalted butter

100 g icing sugar

2 egg yolks

100 g ground almonds

2 Tbsp liqueur, such as orange or pear liqueur, or rum

100 ml/$^1/_2$ cup crème pâtissière (page 120)

450 g flaky pastry (page 118)

For the glaze

1 egg

2 tsp icing sugar

1 Put the butter into the mixer bowl. Sieve over the icing sugar and mix together with the flat beater on speed 1 until creamy. Beat in the egg yolks, one at a time.

2 Mix in the ground almonds and liqueur, then, with the machine still running, beat in the crème pâtissière a tablespoon at a time. Cover and chill until ready to use.

3 Roll out the pastry on a lightly floured surface to a rectangle about 50 x 25 cm. Cut out eight 12-cm rounds, using a small bowl or saucer as a guide. Place four of the rounds on a large greased baking sheet.

4 Spread a quarter of the almond filling in the centre of each pastry round on the baking sheet, leaving a border of about 2 cm all round. Brush the pastry borders with water, then place a second pastry round on top to enclose the filling. Press the edges together to seal, then flute or fork a pattern around the edge. Chill for at least 30 minutes.

5 Preheat the oven to 220°C/Gas Mark 7. Make the glaze by beating the egg and icing sugar together. Brush the tops of the pastries with the glaze, taking care not to allow it to run down the sides of the pastry or it will prevent them from rising evenly.

6 Using a small sharp knife, score the top of the pastry with long curved lines, starting at the centre and ending at the edge, to make a spiral pattern. Make a small hole with a skewer in the centre, to allow steam to escape during cooking.

7 Bake for 20 minutes, or until well-risen and golden brown. Allow to cool for 10 minutes before serving warm or serve cold.

MERINGUES
To make perfect meringues, make sure the eggs are at room temperature and free of any trace of yolk and that the mixer bowl is scrupulously clean, as even a speck of fat can stop the eggs whisking properly.

To make incredibly crisp and light meringue, start whisking the egg whites slowly and turn the speed up gradually until soft peaks form that fall over when the wire whip is removed. After adding the sugar, whisk until the egg whites are shiny and stiff peaks form when the wire whip is removed.

MAKES 24 SMALL MERINGUES

Preparation time: 10 minutes

Cooking time: 3 hours

Attachments used

150 g caster sugar

3 Tbsp water

3 egg whites

Whipped cream, to serve

1 Preheat the oven to 110°C/Gas Mark 1/4. Put the sugar and water in a heavy-based saucepan and heat gently, stirring occasionally until the sugar has dissolved. Once the sugar has completely dissolved, bring the mixture to the boil and boil steadily until a light syrup is formed and a temperature is reached of 115°C. Remove from the heat and reserve.

2 Put the egg whites into the mixer bowl and, using the wire whip, whisk on speed 4, increasing to 8, until the egg whites are stiff and soft peaks are formed.

3 Reduce the speed to 2, slowly pour in the prepared sugar syrup, and continue to whisk until the meringue is glossy and standing in stiff peaks. Spoon into a piping bag fitted with a large star nozzle and pipe 24 small meringues onto a baking sheet lined with non-stick baking parchment. Cook for 2 1/2 to 3 hours until the meringues are dried out and cooked through.

4 Allow to cool, then sandwich the small meringues together with whipped cream.

STRAWBERRY AND PASSION FRUIT PAVLOVA This Australian

meringue dessert was named after the Russian ballerina Anna Pavlova and can be topped with any seasonal fresh fruit.

SERVES AT LEAST 8

Preparation time: 25 minutes

Cooking time: 2 hours

Attachments used

4 medium egg whites

Pinch of salt

225 g caster sugar

1 tsp vinegar

1 tsp cornflour

300 ml/1^{1}/$_{4}$ cups double cream

450 g strawberries (or a mixture of strawberries and raspberries)

2-3 passion fruit

1 Preheat the oven to 180°C/Gas Mark 4. Using the wire whip, on speed 10, whisk the egg whites and salt until stiff. Whisking continuously, add the sugar a tablespoon at a time, beating well after each addition, until all the sugar has been added and the mixture is very stiff and shiny.

2 Sprinkle over the vinegar and the cornflour and whisk on speed 4 for just a few seconds until they are incorporated into the mixture. Pile the mixture onto non-stick baking parchment on a baking sheet and form into a circle approximately 20 cm in diameter.

3 Put the pavlova into the oven, then immediately reduce the heat to 150°C/Gas Mark 2 and leave it to cook for 2 hours. Turn off the oven and leave until it is completely cold.

4 Carefully peel the parchment off the pavlova. You can now either leave the pavlova with the crunchy meringue on top, or turn it upside down and have the crunchy meringue at the bottom, so when you add your cream and fruit you have layers of textures – crunchy meringue, then marshmallow, then cream and then the fruit.

5 Whip the cream in the mixer bowl with the wire whip at speed 4, then increase to speed 8. Place the cream on top and add the strawberries. Scoop the centres from the passion fruit and scatter the passion fruit seeds over the top so that some fall down the sides onto the serving plate.

APFEL STRUDEL

Once you have mastered this wafer-thin strudel pastry, try filling with cherries and cream cheese or a savoury filling of minced meat or bacon mixed with vegetables.

SERVES 8 TO 10

Preparation time: 45 minutes plus 30 minutes standing time

Cooking time: 40 minutes

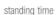

Attachments used

For the pastry

125 g plain flour

Pinch of salt

25 g butter or margarine

1 egg

3 Tbsp hot water

50 g butter, melted

For the filling

1¹/₂ kg cooking apples, peeled and cored

100 g soft light brown sugar

50 g chopped almonds

50 g sultanas

25 g stale white breadcrumbs

¹/₂ tsp ground cinnamon

1 Preheat the oven to 190°C/Gas Mark 5. To make the pastry, sieve the flour and salt into the mixer bowl. Cut the butter or margarine into cubes and add to the flour. Using the flat beater, on speed 1, beat until the butter is incorporated into the flour, then, still on speed 1, gradually add the egg and enough hot water to make a firm dough.

2 Change to the dough hook and knead on speed 4 for 2 minutes until smooth. Transfer the dough to a plastic bag and leave in a warm, draught-free place for 30 minutes.

3 To make the filling, slice the apples into the mixer bowl using the rotary slicer/shredder, with the slicing drum attached, on speed 4. Stir in the sugar, almonds, sultanas, breadcrumbs and cinnamon.

4 Put a clean tea towel on the work surface and sprinkle liberally with flour. Roll the dough out on the tea towel until you have rolled it as thinly as possible. Working quickly, begin to pull the dough over the back of your hands until it is wafer-thin. Do not let the dough go cold, otherwise it will crack.

5 Brush the dough with the melted butter, reserving some for glazing the strudel. Spread the filling evenly over the dough and, using the tea towel, roll it up into a long sausage shape. Transfer to a greased baking sheet and brush the strudel with the remaining melted butter. Cook in the oven for 40 minutes until golden brown and cooked through, then serve warm with cream.

TARTE TATIN (Caramelized apple tart) A delicious French upside-down cake, served in bistros all over the country. Caramelized apples are baked with a pastry topping, then turned upside down to leave the buttery apples showing.

SERVES 8

Preparation time: 50 minutes plus 3 hours chilling time

Cooking time: 1 hour 20 minutes

Attachments used

200 g plain flour

Pinch of salt

225 g chilled butter

50 ml/¼ cup water

1 Tbsp lemon juice

For the filling

1 Tbsp water

175 g caster sugar

80 g butter, cut into pieces

1.5 kg cooking apples, peeled, cored and sliced

1 Sieve the flour and salt into the mixer bowl. Cut 25 g of the butter into cubes and add to the flour, then using the flat beater on speed 2, blend for 30 seconds.

2 Mix the water and lemon juice together. Using the flat beater on speed 2, pour the liquid into the bowl and mix to make a soft, elastic dough.

3 Shape the remaining butter into a rectangle between two sheets of clingfilm or greaseproof paper and gently flatten to a 2-cm thickness.

4 Put the pastry dough onto a lightly floured surface and shape into a circle. Cut a cross in the centre, cutting half the depth of the dough, and open out to form a star. Roll the dough out, keeping the centre four times as thick as the edges. Put the flattened butter into the centre and fold the dough over the top like an envelope, to encase completely.

5 Roll the dough into a 20 x 10-cm rectangle and fold the bottom third up to the centre and the top third down. Seal the edges by pressing with the rolling pin, wrap the pastry in clingfilm and chill in the refrigerator for 30 minutes. Repeat the rolling, folding and chilling process five more times, keeping the sealed edges to the left.

6 Preheat the oven to 180°C/Gas Mark 4. To make the filling, put the water and 100 g of the sugar in a small saucepan and heat over a low heat until it turns to a medium-brown caramel. Once it begins to colour, keep a watchful eye as it will darken quickly. Pour the caramel into the base of a 22-cm nonstick shallow cake tin and cover with the butter and remaining sugar.

7 Arrange the apple pieces around the tin, starting from the outside and working into the centre and wedging them in closely. Place the pastry on top of the apples. Cook for 40 minutes in the oven, or until a knife is easily inserted into the fruit. Leave to cool completely.

APPLE PIE
The all-American apple pie, just like Mom makes. It has pastry underneath and on top. Use a cooking apple, such as Bramleys, as dessert or eating apples become tough and chewy when cooked and tend to lose their flavour.

SERVES 8

Preparation time: 15 minutes plus 30 minutes chilling time

Cooking time: 30 minutes

Attachments used

For the pastry

300 g plain flour

Pinch of salt

2 Tbsp caster sugar

175 g unsalted butter

1 medium egg yolk

1 Tbsp cold water

Extra caster sugar, for sprinkling

For the filling

675 g cooking apples

1 Tbsp plain flour

50 g light soft brown sugar

1 Tbsp softened butter

1 Preheat the oven to 200°C/Gas Mark 6. Sieve the flour and salt into the mixer bowl and stir in the sugar. Cut the butter into cubes and add to the flour together with the egg yolk and cold water. Using the flat beater, on speed 2, beat for about 1 minute or until the mixture comes together and forms a ball in the centre of the bowl. Remove, knead lightly on a lightly floured surface, then wrap and chill in the refrigerator for 30 minutes.

2 To make the filling, peel and core the apples. Attach the slicing drum to the rotary slicer/shredder and, on speed 4, slice the apples into a bowl. Add in the flour and soft brown sugar and stir lightly until the apples are well coated.

3 Knead the pastry on a lightly floured surface until smooth, then roll out half and use to line a deep 20.5-cm pie plate. Dampen the edges with cold water. Spoon in the apple and dot with the butter. Roll the remaining pastry out to form a lid and place on top of the apple. Trim the edges and press lightly together. Use any trimmings to decorate the top of the pie. Brush the top with a little water and sprinkle with caster sugar.

4 Place on a baking sheet and bake in the oven for 25 to 30 minutes, or until the pastry is golden brown. Remove from the oven, sprinkle with more caster sugar to taste and serve with custard, cream or ice cream.

LEMON AND LIME ICE CREAM
Italian gelato is made simply from cream, icing sugar and fresh juice. You could churn it in an ice-cream machine if you have one to give it a creamier texture. Lemon and lime here make a heavenly team.

SERVES 4 TO 6

Preparation time: 15 minutes plus freezing time

Attachments used

2 large lemons

2 limes

175 g icing sugar

584 ml/2¹/₂ cups double cream

1 Using the coarse shredding drum on the rotary slicer/shredder, grate the rind of all the fruit. Using the citrus juicer, on speed 6, juice the fruit and add to a bowl with the sugar and rind.

2 Pour the cream into the mixer bowl, attach the wire whip and pouring shield and whisk the cream, slowly at first, then at speed 6 to 8. Halfway through whipping, add the juice, rind and sugar and mix in until the cream is lightly whipped.

3 Turn into a shallow plastic container and open-freeze until firm, then cover. Before serving, place the container in the refrigerator for half an hour, to soften the ice cream and make it easier to scoop.

MANGO SORBET
A water ice made with ripe mangoes, this sorbet needs beating every hour to break up the large ice crystals, but it should still retain an icy, grainy texture. You can subsitute any really ripe soft fruit for the mango.

SERVES 4

Preparation time: 15 minutes plus freezing time

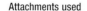

Attachments used

200 ml/1 cup water

150 g granulated sugar

2 large ripe mangoes, peeled, stoned and cubed

Juice of a lemon

2 small or 1 large egg white, lightly beaten

1   Make a syrup by bringing the water and sugar to the boil, stirring to help dissolve the sugar. Simmer for a few minutes, then remove from the heat and allow to cool.

2   Using the strainer, on speed 4, feed the pieces of mango through to obtain a thick purée. Then mix the purée with the syrup and lemon juice.

3   If you are using an ice-cream machine, follow the manufacturer's instructions, adding the egg white for the last 5 minutes of churning. If you do not have an ice cream machine, add the egg whites to the mango purée, then turn into a shallow plastic container.

4   Open-freeze the sorbet, removing every hour and beating to break up the ice crystals.

5   When almost frozen but still liquid in the centre, tip the mixture into the mixer bowl and, using the flat beater, beat on speed 6 to 8 until free of ice crystals.

6   Before serving, place the container in the refrigerator for 1 hour to soften the ice cream and to make it easier to scoop out.

Before straining fruit or vegetables in the strainer, remove any thick skin or rind, such as that on apples and oranges, and any large seeds, hulls or stems. If the fruit or vegetables are very tough you may prefer to cook them before straining, just make sure you adjust any cooking times in the recipes accordingly.

TIRAMISU An Italian dessert of sponge fingers soaked in espresso and topped with soft mascarpone chese, whose name means literally 'pick me up'. The addition of liqueur provides an extra dimension to the coffee flavour.

SERVES 8 TO 10

Preparation time: 15 minutes plus 4 to 6 hours chilling time

Attachments used

8 eggs

110 g icing sugar

1 kg mascarpone (or for a lighter tiramisu: 500 g mascarpone
 and 500 g ricotta cheese)

30 sponge fingers

300 ml/1¼ cups very strong or espresso coffee

60 g cocoa powder

For a liqueur tiramisu

Add ½ Tbsp Marsala, brandy, rum or Amaretto to the coffee

1 Put 4 eggs and 4 egg yolks, the sugar and mascarpone in the mixer bowl and, with the wire whip on speed 2, mix for 30 seconds, increasing to speed 6 for 2 minutes until well combined.

2 Dip 15 sponge fingers into the coffee and use to line the base of a 26 x 15 x 6 cm dish. Cover with half the mascarpone mixture.

3 Dip the remaining sponge fingers into the coffee and layer over the mixture in the dish. Cover with the remaining mascarpone mixture.

4 Sprinkle the top with cocoa powder and refrigerate for 4 to 6 hours.

ZABAGLIONE This sweet creamy dessert is made from Marsala, a sweet Italian fortified wine, and egg yolks and sugar. It can be enjoyed on its own or used as an alternative to cream and served with a dessert or flan.

SERVES 6

Preparation time: 10 minutes

Attachments used

6 egg yolks

100 g icing sugar, sieved

6 Tbsp Marsala

1 Put the egg yolks in the mixer bowl, then add the sugar and Marsala. Using the wire whip, mix on speed 8 for 5 minutes until creamy.

2 Increase the speed to 10 and whisk the mixture for 5 to 7 minutes until it is three times its original volume and only just pourable. Transfer immediately to six tall serving glasses or flutes and serve.

RASPBERRY PARFAIT

A French iced dessert made from an egg custard, to which cream and fruit, chocolate, coffee or a liqueur are added. A parfait is so smooth it can be cut into slices to serve.

SERVES 8

Preparation time: 10 minutes plus 2 hours 20 minutes freezing and standing time

Attachments used

4 eggs

500 g caster sugar

$1/2$ tsp vanilla essence or 2 Tbsp vanilla sugar

Pinch of salt

125 ml/$1/2$ cup double cream

250 g frozen raspberries

1 Put the eggs, sugar, vanilla essence or vanilla sugar and salt into the mixer bowl and, using the wire whip, cream the ingredients together on speed 4 for 1 minute, until well combined. Spoon the mixture into another bowl.

2 Pour the cream into the mixer bowl and, using the wire whip, whisk on speed 8 for 1 minute until thick and peaking. Add the egg mixture and, using the wire whip, mix on speed 2 for 30 seconds.

3 Using the food grinder with the fine grinding plate attached, on speed 4, crush the raspberries into the mixture. Remove the food grinder, replace with the wire whip and mix on speed 2 for 30 seconds until the raspberries are incorporated.

4 Transfer the parfait mixture to 8 individual moulds or one1-litre/4 cup mould and freeze for at least 2 hours until solid. Remove the parfait from the freezer 20 minutes before serving to soften, then unmould onto a serving plate and slice.

FROZEN STRAWBERRY DAIQUIRI
This delicious iced drink is perfect to serve at a cocktail party as it is simple to make but looks and tastes stunning. For a mango daiquiri, substitute fresh mango and mango sorbet for the strawberries.

SERVES 1 TO 2
Preparation time: 5 minutes

Blender used

4 to 6 Tbsp white rum
1/2 tsp lime juice
1 tsp orange juice
3 fresh strawberries
2 scoops strawberry sorbet
Ice cubes
Slices of strawberry and mint leaves, to decorate

1 Combine the rum, lime juice, orange juice, strawberries and the strawberry sorbet in the blender and process at liquefy speed to blend.

2 Pour the daiquiri over ice cubes in two glasses and serve decorated with slices of fresh strawberry and mint leaves.

MARGARITA
A Mexican lime cocktail that tastes wonderful with spicy tortillas and dips. Chill the cocktail glasses before use and coat the rims in a little salt. You can also use Cointreau instead of the triple sec liqueur.

SERVES 4
Preparation time: 10 minutes

Blender used

175 ml/3/4 cup tequila
125 ml/1/2 cup triple sec liqueur
125 ml/1/2 cup fresh lime juice
11/2 Tbsp sugar
24 ice cubes
Lime wedge and salt, to serve

1 Place all the ingredients in the blender. Cover and blend at liquefy speed, pulsing six to eight times for about 15 seconds each time, until slushy.

2 Moisten the rim of the chilled cocktail glasses with a wedge of lime, then turn the glass into a saucer filled with salt to create a salt rim. Pour in the margarita and serve immediately.

CAKES AND COOKIES

THE KITCHENAID BIRTHDAY CAKE
Your mixer is to hand for that special cake, and it couldn't be simpler. You can vary the flavour of this cake and the butter cream according to your preference, and then just decorate accordingly.

SERVES 8 TO 10

Preparation time: 30 minutes

Cooking time: 30 minutes

Attachments used

For the cake

175 g softened unsalted butter or margarine

175 g caster sugar

Grated rind of 1 lemon

3 medium eggs, beaten

175 g self-raising flour

25 g ground almonds

For the butter cream

100 g unsalted butter or margarine

Grated rind of 1 lemon

225 g icing sugar, sieved

1–2 Tbsp lemon juice

50 g toasted flaked almonds

175 g icing sugar

2–3 Tbsp lemon juice

Candles and candle holders

Sugar flowers, or other suitable decoration

1 Preheat the oven to 180°C/Gas Mark 4. Lightly oil and line two 18-cm sandwich tins with greaseproof paper. To make the cake, place the butter or margarine, the sugar and lemon rind in the mixer bowl and, using the flat beater on speed 4, beat until light and fluffy. With the motor running, gradually add the eggs, beating well between each addition, and adding a spoonful of the flour after each addition.

2 When all the eggs have been added, add the remaining flour and the ground almonds, and beat briefly. Add 1 to 2 tablespoons of cooled boiled water if necessary to give a soft dropping consistency. Turn into the prepared tins and level the top.

3 Bake in the oven for 25 to 30 minutes, or until risen and golden brown, and the tops spring back when touched lightly with a fingertip. Remove from the oven and cool slightly, then turn out onto a wire rack. Leave until cold, then discard the lining paper.

4 Make the butter cream by creaming the butter or margarine with the lemon rind in the mixer bowl, using the flat beater on speed 4. Gradually stir in the icing sugar, beating well. Add the lemon juice to give a soft, spreadable consistency.

5 Spread about one-third of the butter cream over one of the cool sponges and place the other sponge on top. Press lightly together.

6 Reserving about 3 tablespoons of the butter cream, spread the remainder round the sides of the cake. Place the toasted almond flakes on a sheet of greaseproof paper, then roll the sides of the cake in the almonds. Put the cake on a serving plate or silver cake board.

7 Spoon the reserved butter cream into a piping bag fitted with a small star nozzle and pipe a border round the edge of the cake.

8 To make the icing, sieve the icing sugar into the mixer bowl, then slowly add the lemon juice, stirring well until a smooth spreadable icing is formed. Pour over the top of the cake and allow to set. Decorate with the sugar flowers or other decorations and, if you like, pipe a greeting on to the set icing.

GUGELHOPF A slender ring-shaped cake popular all over Central Europe, from its origins in Alsace. This version is made with

chocolate and marzipan and looks wonderful dusted with icing sugar just before serving.

SERVES 14

Preparation time: 10 minutes

Cooking time: 35 minutes

Attachments used

225 g butter or margarine

100 g caster sugar

250 g plain flour

1 tsp baking powder

5 eggs, beaten

100 g plain chocolate, chopped small

150 g marzipan, chopped small

4–6 drops bitter almond oil

1 Preheat the oven to 200°C/Gas Mark 6. Butter a 22-cm Gugelhopf tin or fluted ring mould and dust the inside with flour.

2 Put the butter or margarine and sugar in the mixer bowl and, with the flat beater, cream the ingredients on speed 4 for 30 seconds.

3 Mix the flour and baking powder together and, using the flat beater on speed 2, gradually add to the creamed mixture, alternating with the eggs, until all of the ingredients are combined. Stir the chocolate, marzipan and the almond oil into the mixture.

4 Pour into the prepared tin and cook for 35 minutes until cooked through – a skewer inserted into the centre of the cake should come out clean. Turn the cake out onto a wire rack and leave to cool before slicing.

GÂTEAU SAVOIE
A sponge cake from the mountainous region of Savoie in the French Alps, this gâteau has no added fat so it can be whisked with the wire whip, but should be eaten the day it is made.

SERVES 10

Preparation time: 10 minutes

Cooking time: 30 minutes

Attachments used

250 g caster sugar

5 eggs

2 Tbsp water

Pinch of salt

100 g potato flour

100 g plain flour

1 Preheat the oven to 190ºC/Gas Mark 5. Put the sugar in the mixer bowl and add one whole egg. Separate the remaining eggs and add the yolks to the bowl, reserving the egg whites. Add a tablespoon of water and the salt and whisk well with the wire whip on speed 1 for one minute. Increase the speed to 6 and whisk for one further minute until the mixture is white. Transfer to another bowl.

2 Clean the mixer bowl and the wire whip and dry thoroughly, then whisk the egg whites on speed 8 until stiff, add the egg yolk mixture and mix on speed 1 for 30 seconds until combined.

3 Sieve the flours together and whisk into the mixture using the wire whip, on speed 1, for 30 seconds until combined.

4 Butter a deep 20-cm round cake tin and transfer the mixture to the tin. Cook in the oven for 30 to 40 minutes until golden brown and set – a skewer inserted in the centre should come out clean. Turn the cake out onto a wire rack and leave to cool before slicing.

MARBLE CAKE A very simple sponge cake made with two colours of cake mixture, here plain white and chocolate, combined together lightly at the end with a fork to create a marbled effect.

SERVES 12

Preparation time: 10 minutes

Cooking time: 1 hour

Attachments used

250 g butter

250 g caster sugar

4 eggs

500 g plain flour

2 tsp baking powder

750 ml/3 cups milk

2 Tbsp cocoa powder

1 Preheat the oven to 180°C/Gas Mark 4. Grease a deep 20-cm cake tin and set aside. Put the butter, sugar and eggs in the mixer bowl and, with the flat beater, beat the mixture on speed 4 for 1 minute until creamy. Mix the flour and baking powder together and, still using the flat beater, gradually add to the creamed mixture, alternately with the milk. Increase to speed 4 and mix for 2 minutes, until well combined.

2 Spoon two-thirds of the mixture into the prepared cake tin. Add the cocoa powder to the remainder in the mixer and with the flat beater blend on speed 2 for 30 seconds.

3 Pour the cocoa mixture into the cake tin and run a fork through to create a marbled effect. Bake in the oven for 1 hour or until cooked through – a skewer inserted in the centre should come out clean. Leave to cool in the tin for 5 minutes before turning out onto a wire rack to cool completely.

TORTA DI MANDORLE
Almond cakes are made all over Europe, but this Sardinian version is particularly good, with a light whipped sponge covered with a rich almond icing spiked with Amaretto.

SERVES 6

Preparation time: 1 hour

Cooking time: 45 minutes

Attachments used

100 g blanched almonds

1 lemon, preferably unwaxed

4 medium eggs, separated

100 g caster sugar

50 g vanilla sugar

50 g plain flour

1 tsp baking powder

For the topping

50 g blanched almonds

150 g icing sugar

2 Tbsp Amaretto (almond liqueur), optional

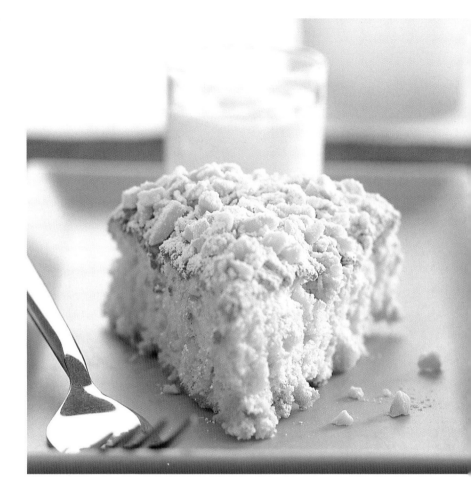

1. Preheat the oven to 190ºC/Gas Mark 4. Lightly oil a 28-cm round cake tin and dust with a little flour. Using the food grinder, fitted with the fine grinding plate, pass the blanched almonds into the mixer bowl on speed 4. Repeat this, to ensure that the almonds are finely chopped, then place in another bowl.

2. Finely grate the lemon rind from half the lemon and squeeze out and reserve the juice. Place the egg yolks into the mixer bowl with the caster and vanilla sugars. Using the wire whip, whisk the mixture on speed 4 until doubled in size and very thick and foamy. Sieve the flour and baking powder into the mixture, then stir in the almonds and lemon rind. Spoon into another bowl.

3. Clean the mixer bowl and the wire whip and dry thoroughly, then whisk the egg whites with 1/2 teaspoon of the reserved lemon juice on speed 8 until stiff and softly peaking. Gradually stir into the egg yolk mixture, then spoon into the prepared cake tin and smooth the top.

4. Tap the tin lightly on the work surface to remove any air bubbles, then bake in the oven for 40 minutes or until the top feels firm to the touch. To test, insert a skewer into the centre of the cake and leave for 30 seconds – if the skewer is clean when removed, the cake is cooked.

Remove from the oven and, when cool, remove from the tin and leave until cold before icing.

5. To make the topping, attach the rotary slicer/shredder with the coarse shredding drum and, on speed 4, chop the almonds. Place in a frying pan and toast lightly. Leave to cool.

6. Sieve the icing sugar into a bowl and gradually stir in 2 tablespoons of the reserved lemon juice and the liqueur if using (or more lemon juice) to form a smooth, spreadable icing. Spread over the cake and sprinkle with the chopped almonds. Leave to set before serving.

APRICOT STREUSEL CAKE
A streusel cake is a cake with a crumbly topping made from butter, sugar, flour and spices. The word streusel comes from the German word for 'sprinkling', and here the topping is sprinkled over apricot halves before baking.

SERVES 12

Preparation time: 20 minutes

Cooking time: 35 minutes

Attachments used

200 g low-fat curd cheese

4 Tbsp milk

4 Tbsp vegetable oil

1 egg

100 g caster sugar

1 Tbsp vanilla sugar

Pinch of salt

400 g plain flour

3 tsp baking powder

For the topping

200 g plain flour

125 g caster sugar

1 Tbsp vanilla sugar

125 g butter

$1/2$ tsp ground cinnamon

Three 400-g cans apricot halves, drained

1 Preheat the oven to 180°C/Gas Mark 4. Put the cheese, milk, oil, egg, caster sugar, vanilla sugar and salt into the mixer bowl and, with the wire whip, combine the ingredients on speed 6 for 30 seconds until fully mixed.

2 Mix the flour and baking powder together and add half to the cheese mixture. Blend with the wire whip for 30 seconds on speed 2.

3 Change the wire whip for the dough hook and add the remaining flour. Knead for 3 minutes on speed 2 until the dough is smooth. Roll the dough out on a lightly greased baking sheet to form a 30-cm circle.

4 To make the topping, put the flour, caster sugar, vanilla sugar and butter in the mixer bowl with the cinnamon and, with the flat beater, mix for 1 to 2 minutes on speed 4, until the mixture is crumbly. Arrange the apricot halves on top of the dough with the rounded side uppermost, then sprinkle the topping evenly over. Cook in the oven for 30 to 35 minutes until golden brown. Serve warm with cream or ice cream.

PFLAUMENKUCHEN

This simple plum cake is a speciality in Bavaria where it is made with tart Italian plums, which are less sweet and juicy than regular plums, and here lies its success. It can be made with any fruit and can also be made without its crumbly cinnamon top.

SERVES 8

Preparation time: 10 minutes

Cooking time: 40 minutes

Attachments used

100 g butter

75 g caster sugar

$^{1}/_{2}$ tsp vanilla essence

1 egg

Pinch of salt

1 Tbsp sour cream

1 tsp grated lemon rind

400 g plain flour

1 tsp baking powder

300 g plums, stoned and halved

For the topping (optional)

2 Tbsp butter

75 g plain flour

75 g caster sugar

$^{1}/_{2}$ tsp ground cinnamon

Whipped cream, to serve

1 Preheat the oven to 190ºC/Gas Mark 5. Put the butter, sugar and vanilla essence into the mixer bowl and, with the flat beater, mix on speed 4 to cream the mixture for 30 seconds. Add the egg, salt, sour cream and lemon rind, and mix on speed 4 for a further 30 seconds. Mix the flour and baking powder together and add to the bowl, mixing on speed 2 for 1 minute until the dough comes together.

2 Lightly grease a shallow 20-cm round cake tin and press the dough into the base. Arrange the plum halves, cut side up, on top of the dough.

3 To make the topping, put the butter, flour, sugar and cinnamon into the mixer bowl and, using the flat beater, cream the mixture on speed 4 for 30 seconds until crumbly. Sprinkle the mixture over the plums evenly and cook in the oven for 30 to 40 minutes until golden brown. Serve warm or cold, topped with freshly whipped cream.

SACHERTORTE
A rich Viennese chocolate cake that needs to be made a day in advance and has a coating of apricot jam and a smooth, dark icing. It traditionally also has the word 'Sacher' piped in chocolate across the top.

SERVES 12

Preparation time: 40 minutes plus overnight standing

Cooking time: 1 hour 10 minutes

Attachments used

130 g plain chocolate

130 g butter

100 g icing sugar, sieved

6 eggs, separated

75 g caster sugar

130 g plain flour

3 Tbsp apricot jam

For the icing

100 g plain chocolate

50 g butter

50 g icing sugar, sieved

2 Tbsp hot water

1 Preheat the oven to 180°C/Gas Mark 4. Heat the chocolate and butter for the cake in a double boiler or in a heatproof bowl over, but not touching, a saucepan of boiling water. Stir and allow to cool a little. Gradually stir in the icing sugar and egg yolks.

2 Put the egg whites in the mixer bowl and, using the wire whip, whisk on speed 8 for 1 minute until they are stiff and peaking. Still using the wire whip on speed 8, add the caster sugar, a tablespoon at a time, until the mixture is peaking again.

3 Transfer the chocolate mixture to a large bowl and carefully stir in a spoonful of the egg whites. Add the remaining egg white to the mixture with alternate spoons of flour, folding in gently.

4 Grease a 23-cm deep cake tin and dust with a little flour. Pour the cake mixture into the tin and cook for 10 minutes with the door slightly open. Reduce the oven temperature to 150°C/Gas Mark 2, and cook for 50 minutes until the cake is cooked through. Remove the cake from the oven, cover with a clean tea towel and leave to cool until the following day.

5 Remove the cake from the tin. Sieve the apricot jam into a small saucepan and warm through. Brush the jam over the top and sides of the cake.

6 Melt the chocolate and butter for the icing in a double boiler or in a heatproof bowl over, but not touching, a saucepan of boiling water and stir in the icing sugar and water. Beat well and leave to stand for 5 minutes before spreading over the top and sides of the cake. Leave to cool before serving.

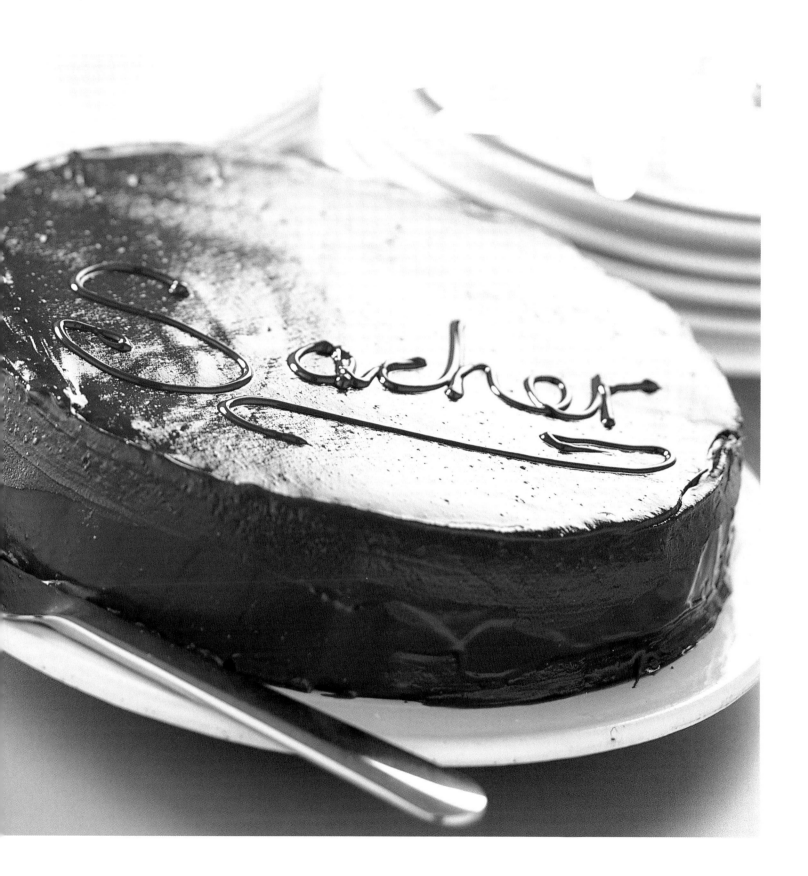

ORANGE CHIFFON CAKE
This very light American cake is made with oil instead of butter. To cut it, you'll need a long serrated knife and to use a gentle sawing motion.

SERVES 6 TO 8

Preparation time: 30 minutes

Cooking time: 1 hour 15 minutes

Attachments used

250 g self-raising flour

3 tsp baking powder

1 tsp salt

300 g caster sugar

125 ml/$^{1}/_{2}$ cup vegetable oil

5 egg yolks, at room temperature

3 Tbsp grated orange zest

175 ml/$^{3}/_{4}$ cup orange juice

8 egg whites, at room temperature

$^{1}/_{2}$ tsp cream of tartar

For the orange glaze

125 ml/$^{1}/_{2}$ cup orange juice

4–5 Tbsp sugar

1 Preheat the oven to 170°C/Gas Mark 3. Sieve the flour, baking powder and salt into the mixer bowl and add the sugar. Make a well in the centre and add the oil, egg yolks and orange zest. Using the flat beater on speed 2, beat for 30 seconds, then stop and scrape the bowl. Add the orange juice, turn to speed 6 and beat for 1 minute. Remove the mixture from the bowl and set aside.

2 Clean the mixer bowl and dry thoroughly, then add the egg whites and the cream of tartar and attach the wire whip. Whisk, on speed 8, until stiff but not dry. Fold the flour mixture into the egg whites, one third at a time, until blended.

3 Pour the batter into an ungreased 25-cm ring mould. Bake in the oven for 55 minutes. Increase the oven temperature to 180°C/Gas Mark 4 and bake for 10 minutes longer. Turn the cake upside down on a wire rack to cool.

4 To make the orange glaze, place the orange juice and sugar in a small saucepan. Bring to the boil over a medium heat and stir until thickened slightly. Remove from the heat and allow to cool.

5 Remove the cake from the mould by gently loosening all the edges with a knife. Place on a serving plate and drizzle the orange glaze over the top.

WALNUT CAKE WITH SYRUP
This Greek cake, made with walnuts and coated with a cinnamon-sugar syrup, is baked to be enjoyed with a small cup of strong Greek coffee.

SERVES 8

Preparation time: 1 hour

Cooking time: 1 hour 10 minutes

Attachments used

500 g walnuts

4 slices (about 125 g) day-old white bread, crusts discarded

125 g unsalted butter

4 medium eggs, separated

130 g caster sugar

1¹/2 Tbsp baking powder

1 Tbsp ground cinnamon

150 ml/²/₃ cup cognac

For the syrup

400 g sugar

600 ml/ 2¹/2 cups water

Cinnamon stick, lightly bashed

Large pieces of thinly pared lemon rind

1 Preheat the oven to 180°C/Gas Mark 4. Lightly oil and line a 20.5-cm deep cake tin with greaseproof paper. With the coarse grinding plate on the grinder, on speed 4, grind the nuts and then the bread into crumbs. Reserve both separately.

2 Place the butter in the mixer bowl. Using the flat beater, on speed 6, beat until soft and creamy. Add the egg yolks one at a time, beating well after each addition. When all the egg yolks have been added, stir in the sugar and continue to beat until the mixture is well combined.

3 Sieve the baking powder into the mixture, then add the breadcrumbs and the ground cinnamon. Beat for 1 minute until well mixed. Turn into another bowl.

4 Clean the mixer bowl and dry thoroughly then, using the wire whip, on speed 10, whisk the egg whites until stiff and standing in peaks. Carefully stir into the creamed mixture alternately with the chopped walnuts and the cognac.

5 Stir gently until thoroughly mixed, then spoon into the prepared cake tin and level the top. Bake in the oven for 1 hour. Remove and allow to cool before taking out of the tin.

6 To make the syrup, place the sugar and the water in a heavy-based saucepan and heat gently until the sugar has dissolved. Add the cinnamon stick and lemon rind and bring to the boil. Boil steadily for 5 minutes or until a light syrup is formed. Remove the cinnamon stick and lemon rind. Pour the warm syrup over the cake and leave until cold before serving.

BUÑUELOS DE MANZANA
Irresistible apple fritters are made with whole pieces of apple, marinated in an aniseed liqueur and deep-fried in batter until crisp and golden. They need to be eaten as soon as they are cooked, dusted with sugar.

MAKES 32

Preparation time: 40 minutes plus 1 hour standing time

Cooking time: 5 minutes

Attachments used

3 Tbsp anisette or Pernod

100 g caster sugar

8 eating apples, peeled, cored, and cut into rings

4 eggs

300 ml/1¹/₄ cups milk

300 g plain flour

1 packet (7 g) active dry yeast

2 tsp salt

2 Tbsp plain flour, for coating

Oil, for deep-frying

Icing sugar, for dusting

1 Mix the anisette and sugar together in a bowl and toss the apple rings into the mixture. Set aside for 30 minutes.

2 Put the eggs and milk in the mixer bowl and, with the flat beater, mix on speed 2 for 30 seconds. Add the flour, yeast and salt, and mix for 1 minute on speed 4. Leave the batter to rest for an hour.

3 Drain the apples and toss them in the coating flour, then roll in the batter to coat them well.

4 Heat a deep pan of oil to 180°C and cook the apples in four batches for 1 minute until golden brown. Remove from the oil with a slotted spoon, drain on kitchen paper and keep warm while cooking the remaining apples. Dust the fritters with icing sugar and serve warm.

COCONUT MACAROONS

These little macaroons, a favourite of French pâtisseries, are made from coconut rather than the more usual ground almonds. They can be served with a dessert wine or an ice cream or mousse.

MAKES ABOUT 30 MACAROONS

Preparation time: 10 minutes

Cooking time: 35 minutes

Attachments used

4 egg whites

1/4 tsp cream of tartar

250 g caster sugar

1 tsp lemon juice or white wine vinegar

1 tsp vanilla essence

250 g desiccated coconut

1   Preheat the oven to 150ºC/Gas Mark 2. Line two baking sheets with non-stick baking parchment.

2   Using the wire whip on speed 4, beat the egg whites until frothy. Add the cream of tartar and beat on speed 10 until stiff peaks form. Whisking continuously, add the sugar 2 tablespoons at a time, beating well after each addition, until all the sugar has been added and the mixture is very stiff and shiny.

3   Sprinkle the lemon juice or vinegar, vanilla essence and coconut over the meringue mixture. Whisk on speed 4 for just a few seconds until incorporated into the mixture.

4   Drop heaped teaspoons of the mixture onto the prepared baking sheets, spacing them slightly apart. Bake for 30 to 35 minutes, until the macaroons are light golden and the insides are still slightly soft.

5   Leave on the baking sheets for 5 minutes, then transfer to a wire rack to cool. Store in an airtight container.

SHORTBREAD

This rich Scottish biscuit is traditionally cut into wedges called 'petticoat tails'. For an even shorter texture, you can substitute 75 g of the flour for an equal amount of ground rice or rice flour.

MAKES 16 WEDGES

Preparation time: 10 minutes

Cooking time: 30 minutes

Attachments used

60 g icing sugar

60 g caster sugar

175 g butter, softened

300 g plain flour

1   Preheat the oven to 150ºC/Gas Mark 2. Sieve the icing sugar into the mixer bowl. Add the caster sugar and butter and use the flat beater, on speed 1, to mix them together. Increase to speed 6 and cream the mixture until it is pale and fluffy.

2   Sieve the flour over the creamed mixture and mix on speed 2 until the mixture resembles large breadcrumbs.

3   Gather the dough together with your hands and divide equally between two 20-cm loose-bottomed cake tins, lightly pressing it until even with the back of a spoon. Using a fork, mark a pattern around the edges, then lightly prick the surface all over.

4   Bake for 30 minutes, or until the shortbread is a pale golden colour, rotating the tins halfway through cooking. Mark the surface of each into eight wedges while the shortbread is still warm and soft.

5   Leave to cool in the tins on a wire rack, then remove the rims from the tins, cut the shortbread into wedges and store in an airtight container.

LEBKUCHEN
There are lots of varieties of these little German cakes made with honey and spices and glazed after baking.

A little like gingerbread, they are often served as a Christmas treat.

MAKES 24

Preparation time: 35 minutes plus at least 8 hours chilling time

Cooking time: 30 minutes

Attachments used

250 ml/1 cup clear honey

175 g dark brown sugar

1 egg, beaten

1 Tbsp lemon juice

1 tsp grated lemon rind

300 g plain flour

1 tsp ground cinnamon

$1/2$ tsp ground allspice

$1/2$ tsp ground cloves

$1/2$ tsp ground nutmeg

$1/2$ tsp salt

$1/2$ tsp baking powder

50 g candied chopped lemon

50 g chopped almonds

Rice paper or baking parchment paper

12 glacé cherries, halved, for decoration

175 g blanched almonds, for decoration

100 g icing sugar, to glaze

2–3 Tbsp rum, to glaze

1 Heat the honey in a saucepan until it begins to bubble. Remove from the heat and stir in the brown sugar, egg, lemon juice and rind and set aside.

2 Put the flour, spices, salt and baking powder into the mixer bowl. With the flat beater, on speed 2, add the honey mixture and mix until well blended. Stir in the candied lemon and chopped almonds and leave to stand in the refrigerator for at least 8 hours and up to 24 hours if possible.

3 Preheat the oven to 190ºC/Gas Mark 5. Working with a quarter of the dough at a time, and keeping the remainder refrigerated, roll the dough out on a heavily floured work surface to a 1-cm thickness. Cut 9-cm rounds of rice paper or baking parchment paper and space 4 cm apart on a baking sheet.

4 Cut out 6.5-cm rounds from the dough and place one onto each paper base. Put a cherry half into the centre of each and arrange five almonds around the cherry to represent flower petals. Cook in two batches in the oven for 12 to 15 minutes each batch. Repeat with the remaining dough.

5 Make up the glaze by mixing the icing sugar and rum and spread over the cakes after cooking. Leave to cool.

TOPFENKOLATSCHE
These Austrian pastries are made with cream cheese rather than curd cheese, though you could use either. A wonderful sweet breakfast or afternoon treat.

MAKES 10

Preparation time: 1 hour, plus 2 hours 15 minutes standing time

Cooking time: 30 minutes

Attachments used

For the pastry
400 g plain flour
Pinch of salt
1 packet (7 g) active dry yeast
120 ml/$\frac{1}{2}$ cup warm milk
2 Tbsp caster sugar
1 egg
2 Tbsp butter, melted

For the filling
2 Tbsp butter
225 g cream cheese
2 eggs, separated
100 g caster sugar
Grated rind of 1 lemon
1 Tbsp raisins

1 egg white, lightly beaten, for brushing
2 Tbsp chopped almonds

1 Sieve the flour and salt for the pastry into the mixer bowl and add the yeast, warm milk, sugar and egg. With the dough hook, mix on speed 4 for 1 minute until well blended. Changing to speed 2, add the melted butter in a stream. Cover the bowl and leave to stand for 1 hour 30 minutes, until doubled in size.

2 Put the dough on a lightly floured work surface and roll out to a 1-cm thickness. Cut into 7-cm squares and transfer to a baking sheet.

3 To make the filling, put the butter, cream cheese, egg yolks, sugar, lemon rind and raisins in the mixer bowl, fit the flat beater and mix on speed 4 for 30 seconds until soft. Transfer to a small bowl.

4 Clean the mixer bowl and dry thoroughly, then attach the wire whip and on speed 8 whisk the egg whites until stiff. Add the cream cheese mixture and blend with the flat beater on speed 2 until combined.

5 Put a tablespoon of filling into the centre of each pastry square and fold the corners in to cover the filling, sealing the edges by pinching together. Leave to rise in a warm, draught-free place for 45 minutes.

6 Heat the oven to 180°C/Gas Mark 4. Brush the pastries with egg white and sprinkle the almonds on top. Cook for 30 minutes until well browned.

BLUEBERRY MUFFINS

These all-American muffins are so quick to prepare that you can bake them when you wake up for a weekend breakfast. Eat them when fresh and try making a batch using raspberries instead of blueberries.

MAKES 16

Preparation time: 10 minutes

Cooking time: 30 minutes

Attachments used

275 g blueberries

225 g plain flour

2$^{1}/_{2}$ tsp baking powder

$^{1}/_{2}$ tsp salt

$^{1}/_{4}$ tsp ground nutmeg

175 g caster sugar

2 eggs

175 ml/$^{3}/_{4}$ cup milk

115 g butter, melted

Grated rind of 1 orange

1 tsp vanilla essence

50 g granulated sugar

$^{1}/_{4}$ tsp ground nutmeg

1 Preheat the oven to 190ºC/Gas Mark 5. Line two muffin tins with 16 paper cases or lightly grease with butter.

2 Mash about 50 of the blueberries with a potato masher or fork. Sieve the flour, baking powder, salt and nutmeg into the mixer bowl. Stir in the sugar and make a well in the centre.

3 With the flat beater, on speed 2, beat the eggs, milk, melted butter, orange rind, vanilla essence and mashed blueberries into the flour, mixing for 30 seconds and being careful not to overmix. Gently mix in the remaining blueberries and spoon the mixture into the prepared tins, almost filling to the top with mixture.

4 Mix the granulated sugar and ground nutmeg together and sprinkle over the muffins. Cook in the oven for 25 to 30 minutes until risen and golden. Remove from the oven and cool in the tin for 5 minutes before transferring to a wire rack to cool.

SULTANA SCONES

Scones served with jam and spoonfuls of whipped or clotted cream are an essential part of British afternoon tea and are easy and quick to make. For a change, you could replace the raisins with ready-to-eat dried apricots or dried cranberries.

MAKES 8

Preparation time: 10 minutes

Cooking time: 10 minutes

Attachments used

225 g self-raising flour

Pinch of salt

50 g unsalted butter or margarine

2 Tbsp caster sugar

50 g sultanas

About 150 ml/^{2}/$_3$ cup milk

Milk, to glaze

Butter or cream and jam, to serve

1 Preheat the oven to 230°C/Gas Mark 8. Lightly oil a baking sheet. Sieve the flour and salt into the mixer bowl and add the butter or margarine, the sugar and sultanas.

2 Using the flat beater, on speed 2, beat until the butter or margarine has been rubbed in. Still on speed 2, gradually pour in the milk until the mixture comes together and forms a ball in the centre of the bowl.

3 Turn out onto a very lightly floured surface and knead briefly to remove any cracks. Gently roll out to 2 cm thick and cut out 2-cm rounds with a pastry cutter dipped into flour.

4 Place on the oiled baking sheet and brush the tops with a little milk. Bake in the oven for 8 to 10 minutes, or until well risen and golden brown. Serve with butter or cream and jam.

DOUBLE CHOCOLATE BROWNIES
These sumptuous brownies can be cut into small squares for a snack or served in larger pieces with ice cream and a drizzle of melted chocolate for dessert.

MAKES ABOUT 20 SQUARES

Preparation time: 20 minutes

Cooking time: 30 minutes

Attachments used

300 g luxury dark chocolate

200 g butter

200 g caster sugar

3 eggs

2 Tbsp Frangelico liqueur (optional)

75 g self-raising flour

75 g roasted hazelnuts, chopped

100 g white chocolate chips

1 Preheat the oven to 190°C/Gas Mark 5. Grease and line the base of a 23-cm square baking tin with baking parchment.

2 Break the chocolate into small pieces and place in a double boiler or in a heatproof bowl over, but not touching, a saucepan of boiling water. Add the butter and heat until melted.

3 Beat the sugar and eggs thoroughly using the flat beater on speed 4, then with the motor still running, gradually drizzle in the melted chocolate mixture and the Frangelico if you are using it. Allow to cool slightly, then add the flour and hazelnuts and mix with the flat beater on speed 4 to combine. Finally, add the white chocolate chips and fold in briefly on speed 2.

4 Pour the mixture into the prepared tin and bake for about 25 to 30 minutes or until just set. Remove from the oven and allow to cool in the tin.

SPEKULATIUS
Spicy Austrian biscuits, flavoured with cinnamon and almonds and cut into star shapes for Christmas, make enchanting gifts or decorations. Dust again with icing sugar before serving.

MAKES 30

Preparation time: 15 minutes

Cooking time: 30 minutes

Attachments used

3 large egg whites

250 g icing sugar, sieved

2 tsp vanilla essence

1 tsp ground cinnamon

2 drops almond essence

400 g ground almonds

1–2 tsp cold water

Icing sugar, for icing and dusting

1 Preheat the oven to 140ºC/Gas Mark 1. Line a baking sheet with baking parchment. Put the egg whites into the mixer bowl and using the wire whip, whisk the egg whites on speed 8 until stiff and peaking. Remove 1 heaped tablespoon of egg white for glazing and reserve. Reduce to speed 2 and stir in the icing sugar, 1 to 2 tablespoons at a time.

2 Add the vanilla essence, ground cinnamon, almond essence and half of the ground almonds to the mixture, using the wire whip on speed 2. Add enough of the remaining almonds to give a fairly stiff dough.

3 Dust a work surface with icing sugar and roll the dough out to 5-mm thickness. Using a star-shaped cookie cutter, cut stars from the dough, kneading and rerolling until it has all been used up.

4 Transfer the biscuits to the baking sheet. Mix the reserved egg white with the cold water and brush over the top of the biscuits. Cook in the oven for 25 to 30 minutes, then cool on a wire rack.

5 Once cooled, spread with white icing or dust the cookies with icing sugar just before serving. Store in an airtight container until ready to eat.

BISCOTTI
Small Italian almond biscuits that are hard and crunchy and made to be dipped into a glass of vin santo, Tuscan dessert wine, at the end of a special meal.

MAKES ABOUT 60

Preparation time: 15 minutes

Cooking time: 35 minutes

200 g slivered almonds

2 tsp butter, for greasing

3 medium eggs, separated

250 g caster sugar

Pinch of salt

Grated rind of 1 lemon

400 g plain flour

3 tsp baking powder

Attachments used

1 Preheat the oven to 180°C/Gas Mark 4. Place the almonds on a non-stick baking sheet and toast in the preheated oven for 5 to 10 minutes or until golden. Remove and cool. Lightly grease two baking sheets with butter.

2 Put the egg yolks and sugar into the mixer bowl and fit the flat beater. Beat the mixture on speed 4 for 30 seconds. Transfer to another bowl.

3 Clean the mixer bowl and dry thoroughly, then attach the wire whip and whisk the egg whites and salt on speed 8 until peaking. Still using the wire whip, on speed 4, gradually add the egg yolk mixture until fully incorporated. Grate the rind of the lemon into the mixture, and add the toasted almonds. Fit the dough hook, and mix the dough on speed 4 for 30 seconds. Add the flour, baking powder and butter. Continue to mix on speed 4 for a further minute to knead the dough.

4 Place the dough on a lightly floured surface and roll into four, 2 cm wide sausage shapes. Transfer to the baking sheets and bake in the preheated oven for 15 minutes until the edges have begun to turn golden brown.

5 Remove from the oven and immediately cut into 1-cm thick slices, cutting on the diagonal. Cool on wire cooling racks. Store once cold in an airtight container.